THE
PROBLEM
WITH
MEN

Also by Richard Herring

Emergency Questions: 1001 Conversation
Starters for Every Occasion

RICHARD HERRING

THE

PROBLEM

WITH

MEN

sphere

SPHERE

First published in Great Britain in 2020 by Sphere

1 3 5 7 9 10 8 6 4 2

The Male Feminist stand-up on p66 written and performed in 2019 by Bill Burr as
part of the Netflix stand-up special of *Bill Burr: Paper Tiger.*

A CIP catalogue record for this book is available from the British Library.

ISBN 978-0-7515-8145-4

Typeset in Bembo by M Rules
Printed and bound in Great Britain by Clays Ltd, Elcograf S.p.A.

Papers used by Sphere are from well-managed forests
and other responsible sources.

Sphere
An imprint of
Little, Brown Book Group
Carmelite House
50 Victoria Embankment
London EC4Y 0DZ

An Hachette UK Company
www.hachette.co.uk

www.littlebrown.co.uk

For Catie, Phoebe and Ernie
For helping me to be a better man

CONTENTS

THE PROBLEM WITH MEN

INTRODUCTION

'When's International Men's Day?'

I don't remember which year I first saw this question raised on Twitter, but I can tell you the date. It was March 8th.

I know that because March 8th is International Women's Day.

You might be wondering why anyone would ask that question on, according to the International Women's Day website: 'a global day celebrating the social, economic, cultural and political achievements of women. The day also marks a call to action for accelerating women's equality'.

It's surely not unreasonable to set aside twenty-four hours (out of the 8,760 annually available) to celebrate slightly more than 50 per cent of the world's population.

Let's be generous and say that the people asking 'When's International Men's Day?' on International Women's Day are attempting to make some kind of a joke. It's a clever and subtle one, though, so I feel I will have to walk you through it . . .

In just four words[1] they are pointing out that even though International Women's Day supposedly promotes equality, there is (presumably) no equivalent for men? That's not very balanced, is it? It's a bit sexist when you think about it.

On top of that is the inference that there could NEVER be a day to venerate men, due to political correctness gone mad. It wouldn't even be allowed, because men are the underclass in today's topsy-turvy world.

It is, you have to admit, a brilliant and concise piece of social satire, worthy of Jonathan Swift.

If it weren't for one tiny thing.

There *is* an International Men's Day.

It's on November 19th.

Still, you have to admire the confidence that allows someone to fire the fated question out into the world without even pausing to check Google. You know, just to ensure that they don't end up looking like an idiot.

Initially I found this amusing for its own sake – like you would a clown swinging to hit someone with a custard pie, but missing and hitting themselves in the face.

On top of this, though, I noticed that if you were foolish enough to search for the phrase 'International Men's Day' on Twitter, you would find thousands of people moved to make the exact same 'joke', all thinking they were making some insightful and original point. Not one of them was insecure

1   As Polonius says in *Hamlet*, 'Brevity is the soul of wit'. That's six words, Shakespeare, so they're funnier than you, by your own standards.

enough to check out if it was an interesting or unique thought, let alone whether the basic assumption behind the question held true.

You have to understand this was the early 2010s when we had no idea that confident idiots with no regard for facts would soon be running the world. So we could laugh, rather than crawl under a table and try to crush our brains in with a potato masher.

In hindsight, we should have spotted the greater implications for humanity. This simple enough question contained the kernel of truth about the over-sensitive, butt-hurt babies who were soon to have far too much control in the world. This was page one of their one-page playbook – deflect criticism by flipping the narrative to manufacture injustice. If only we'd paid attention and spotted it sooner.

I will admit that when I started noticing the 'When's International Men's Day?' trope I was no fan of the idea of an International Men's Day. It seemed to me like a knee-jerk reaction to International Women's Day designed solely to undermine it. To my mind it made the men complaining about it look a bit pathetic (not just because there actually was a day already[1], but also because it was such a babyish way to behave). Equally, though, in that moment I wasn't really thinking about politics or feminism or the crisis in masculinity. I just thought it might be funny to spend 'International

---

1   On November 19th.

"When's International Men's Day?" Day' (as I began to view it) searching Twitter for everyone who asked this question and politely telling them the answer: November 19th. I did this partly to see how they responded, partly to show everyone else how ubiquitous this inappropriate (on this one day) question was and partly in the hope that if I let everyone know, then maybe no one would ask the question ever again.

Of course, by doing this I was setting up an even bigger joke: an even more custardy custard pie that was destined for my own face. That pie would swing and hit me every few seconds for twenty-four hours on an annual basis for almost a decade.

I had willingly made myself into a modern-day King Cnut.[1] I thought I had the power to turn back the waves (of idiots, in my case). But, like him, I would end up drenched (in stupidity, in my case). My twenty-four-hour self-employment as a twat-seeking search engine would leave me overwhelmed, delirious and, by around about 6 p.m. on the day in question, lead to me losing all semblance of politeness or chivalry. Was this social media breakdown merely for comic affect or was it genuine? Even I wasn't sure. My replies became more befuddled, unreasonable and insane. It was fun for people to spectate. It was not fun to be at the centre of this hurricane of twats.

It proved amusing to most. A few were irritated by the

---

1   This is the correct original spelling of the name of the monarch who is erroneously and much less amusingly more often known as Canute.

relentlessness and unfollowed or muted me. Pretty quickly I upset some meninists who thought I was undermining the importance of their day (which they said wasn't a knee-jerk reaction to women having a day and actually dealt with important issues like male depression and suicide) and I also annoyed some feminists who thought I was making International Women's Day about myself, a man. I have some sympathy with both criticisms, and at least I achieved the impossible and united the meninists and feminists – even if it was in hatred of me.

I wasn't trying to be irksome, but those who were affronted or bored generally failed to recognise the joke was on me. It was a car crash of tedium and self-owned petard-hoisting, though I'd hoped that some at least could admire my patience and resilience.

It took me six years to realise that maybe people would make a donation to charity in return for my dogged and ridiculous dedication. A sort of sponsored trolling. Even if, arguably, I was trolling trolls. But a troll-troller is still a troll.

In 2017, I encouraged my Twitter followers to spur me on by giving money to Refuge, a fantastic enterprise that helps women, children and men who live in fear of violence. The response was beyond my wildest dreams: donations flooded in. I was raising thousands of pounds an hour. I had invented a philosopher's stone that turned idiocy (both the questioners' and my own) into gold.

In the end, I would take on this impossible challenge for

nine consecutive International Women's Days. Like Sam Beckett in *Quantum Leap* (though it could equally have been something created by the guy who wrote *Waiting For Godot*), I hoped that each completed year would be my leap home. This turned out to be a mission that could not be completed.

The mental strain was becoming too much, but I was also forced to acknowledge what I really knew from the start. This task was too big for Twitter. The issues that fuelled the anger and resentment behind the question, and its responses, were bigger than the answer to this one question that no one actually wanted the answer to.

I wondered if I could do better if I allowed myself more than 280 characters and asked more than one question.

Maybe more important than knowing when International Men's Day is[1] is asking: Is International Men's Day something worth celebrating? If so, what should it be about and how could the world be convinced to join in? What does it even mean to be a man in the twenty-first century and who is to blame for the (few?) bad cards we've been dealt? Are women the enemies of the male sex or our friends, lovers and allies? If we want equality, why does feminism, which promises exactly that, scare and infuriate so many?

I will attempt to answer 19 NOVel questions,[2] in the hope

---

1 It's on November 19th.
2 Many of them aren't novel, but saying 19 pertinent questions doesn't cleverly reveal the date of International Men's Day. Do you see what I did there? My editor didn't. Hence this over-explained footnote.

that I can finally achieve my dream and stop anyone ever asking 'When's International Men's Day?', even if it's just that one day of the year when it's invariably and inappropriately asked.

Or maybe I will fail again and just prove what everyone assumed from the start, that I am a massive Cnut.

@█████████[1] When is it international men's day? Or am I once again being positively discriminated against . . .

| @Herring1967 It's November 19th

@████████ When is it International Men's Day? It's not easy being a man. *awaits derisory laughter from women*

| @Herring1967 It's on November 19th

@████████ Pretty sexist how there's no international men's day . . . AHA!

| @Herring1967 It's on November 19th. AHA!

@████████ So errr . . . when's international mens day?? Will there be a parade . . .

@Herring1967 It's on nov 19. Plenty of time to organise a parade.

@████████ does international men's day exist? Bet we'd get moaned at for pushing that

@Herring1967 It does. You wouldn't. It's November 19th

@████████ is there an international men's day?

| @Herring1967 Yes it's November 19th

---

1 These are all real tweets that I have received over the years, but I've blanked out their Twitter handles as I think they have suffered enough.

| @▆▆▆▆ Thanks
| @Herring1967 No need to thank me. I'm just
| doing my job.

@Herring1967 I am like a superhero and my powers
are knowing when IMD is and telling people who don't
know. It's November 19th.

1

WHAT'S WRONG WITH ASKING WHEN INTERNATIONAL MEN'S DAY IS ON INTERNATIONAL WOMEN'S DAY?

Everything!

Everything is wrong with it.

It's ignorant, it's impolite, it's inappropriate and, worst of all, it just makes the person posing the question look like a lazy and possibly misogynist idiot.

And not just because there *is* an International Men's Day and it's on November 19th.

When people do this they're trying to steal focus from something that is *not* about them in order to make it about themselves. And yes, we'll get on to the glaring hypocrisy of me saying that soon enough.

Asking the aforementioned question on International Women's Day is blatantly self-centred and babyish, manufacturing outrage from a position of superiority. It's the same impulse that makes children question having two separate days set aside every year to celebrate mothers and fathers by asking, 'When will there be a Children's Day?' Though at least children have the excuse of being children and thus naturally self-obsessed and unable to spot that the world pretty much revolves around them already.

Delightfully (and to keep this analogy spot on) there is also an International Children's Day. It's on June 1, and is dedicated to all those children worldwide living in terrible circumstances. That won't assuage your complaining spawn, of course. Because, like the grown-up children questioning International Women's Day, they are actually asking, 'When's MY day? When will someone make me breakfast and let me put my feet up and watch the telly? When will that happen? You know, apart from every single fucking day?'

Asking 'When's International Men's Day?' on International Women's Day is like going to someone else's birthday party and, instead of bringing them a present and singing 'Happy Birthday', smashing up all their gifts with a baseball bat and shouting, 'When is it MY birthday? Why aren't I getting presents? Why doesn't anyone care about ME?'

When I was six, I went to my next-door neighbour Clare Allen's birthday party and we played pass the parcel and somehow (and I still suspect some kind of scam, given that Clare's mum was operating the music) Clare won and got the bag of sweets in the middle and I LOST MY SHIT. I wouldn't calm down about the unfairness of it all until Mrs Allen gave me a mini Mars Bar.

I had made a valid point about the injustice of no one celebrating my birthday at this party (just because it wasn't my birthday) and I ate my sweet confection of victory.

But was there anyone at that party who didn't conclude I was a total dick? Was anyone thinking, 'I can't wait till Richard's birthday comes along and we can really celebrate what a fine fellow he is'? Or did it make them less likely to show enthusiasm or show up on July 12th?[1]

Maybe you're thinking: 'Come on, the International Men's Day question is just a joke. We've all had enough of those sanctimonious social-justice warriors who ruin our lives telling us what we're meant to think and want to stop us having fun. Let's wind them up and see how cross we can make them.'

I get it. I've often attempted to wind those people up, too. I'm a comedian. Mischief is my job. But comedy is a serious business and you have to make sure your prank is solid or the comedy bomb can explode in your own face.

If I went on stage on International Women's Day and said, 'So when's International Men's Day?', someone would heckle, 'It's November 19th.'

And I would have no response and the audience would sense my weakness and the night would be lost. Because this

---

1 Mark it in your diary, folks. Though, unbelievably, the UN have declared it Malala Day. When's it Richard Herring Day?

is not a good joke. It ceases to work because there is a day.[1]

Some feel that they are righteously pointing out liberal hypocrisy. If women want an equal world, then surely it is wrong that they have a day and men don't. That's not equal.

This argument falters somewhat because (and forgive me if I have already pointed this out) there is an International Men's Day and it's on November 19th, but even if there wasn't – THAT'S NOT HOW EQUALITY WORKS.

We have an International Women's Day to acknowledge the ways that society is unequal and to attempt to address that. I can't tell you the number of times that women have wearily tweeted their own answer to the question 'When's International Men's Day?' : 'It's every *other* day of the year.'[2]

Asking 'When's International Men's Day?' on International Women's Day is like asking 'When's White History Month?' during Black History Month.[3] It's like waking up on 18th October and finding out it's Anti-Slavery Day and asking, 'When's it Pro-Slavery Day? When do we have a day to look at things from the slave owners' point of view? Or is that not "politically correct" #equality.' It's like waiting for World AIDS Day to come along on December 1st and tweeting, 'I don't have AIDS. Why isn't there a non-AIDS day? When will there be a day for me?'

It's true that men suffer from inequality in certain areas.

---

1   On November 19th
2   This is factually incorrect. The actual answer is November 19th.
3   See Chapter 16.

That's one of the reasons they have an International Men's Day[1] – so you can talk about them then. If you genuinely care about that day (and we'll talk later about whether any of the people asking the question really do) then it's counterproductive to bring it up on March 8th.

Talking about men's issues on International Women's Day isn't going to make people sympathetic. Quite the opposite. Because you're acting like six-year-old Richard Herring throwing a tantrum about not winning some jelly babies at someone else's party.

If you behave like a dick on everyone else's birthday, then it shouldn't surprise you if they're not that interested in celebrating yours.

---

1 On November 19th

@████████ Yeah but you wouldn't have an international mans day because that would be sexist and discriminatory

> @Herring1967 Apart from the one on November 19th

@████████ Hang on when the fuck is it international mans day?!

> @Herring1967 Fucking November the fucking 19th

@████████ imagine the uproar if there was an 'international men's day' . . .

> @Herring1967 There would be (and is in fact) none. It's Nov 19th

@████████ Is there international men's day? If not I call sexism.

> @Herring1967 there is. It's Nov 19. So no sexism in the world at all. Phew.

@████████ International women day today I hear! Bet my right cock that there isn't International Men Day at all.

> @Herring1967 You've lost your right cock. It's Nov 19. Hold on tight to the left one.

@█████ When is International Men's Day? I forget . . .

@Herring1967 It's Nov 19. Maybe write it down so you'll remember

2

IS IT DEFINITELY SEXIST TO ASK ABOUT INTERNATIONAL MEN'S DAY ON INTERNATIONAL WOMEN'S DAY?

Oh God, no. Of course not. Not everyone who goes on about International Men's Day on International Women's Day is sexist! It might be true that everyone who is sexist goes on about International Men's Day on International Women's Day, but there are lots of other reasons to do it too . . .

Loads.

I wish I had been given a longer book so I could list them all.

Let's just do one.

Um.

Hold on, I've got it.

Some people just enjoy being wilfully contrary.[1] They believe absolutely in freedom of speech and the right to say the things that are unsayable. Even when literally thousands of people are already saying them. So many that it's not actually physically possible to respond to all of them, even if you set a whole day aside and do nothing else.

We need these heroic and noble contrarians to keep society on its tracks, to relentlessly contradict the opinions of experts or anyone who has bothered to think about stuff for a second and champion neglected and redundant causes. It doesn't matter if they are causes that no one could possibly care about. All that matters is that the unsayable is said. Even if the unsayable is stupid and upsets people for no real reason. This is part of a greater freedom. The right to be a fucking wazzock. The greatest of the human rights, along with the right to bear arms and the right to freedom of speech (as long as you're not forced to listen to anyone's replies).

It's not about political correctness or sexism. Wazzocks just want balance to the Universe, ying and yang.[2]

I'm with them all the way. And also fully oppose them. It's the wazzock way. However I believe none of them are doing it thoroughly enough. They're only being partially contrary. If they're all about being opposite then they should be tweeting 'International Women's Day? When's National Men's Night?'

---

1 I know I don't.
2 I am aware it is yin and yang, but alas the wazzocks are not.

It must be annoying for the wazzocks that some of their work fearlessly stating the opposite means they occasionally get lumped together with people who enjoy spouting sexist and racist nonsense. People only notice the wazzocks tweeting about International Men's Day or White History Month and make terrible assumptions based solely on the awful character of everyone else asking those questions. They don't check the rest of the wazzock's Twitter feed to see them writing:

'Christmas Day? Why don't we celebrate Satan's birthday? Double standards.'

'Easter? What about Wester? Or wouldn't that be allowed?'

'Groundhog Day? When do we get Skyshare Day?'

'Every dog has its day? When will every cat get its day?[1] That's cattist.'

'Bath Night? When's Toilet Day?'[2]

'Darren Day? Where's Sharon Day?'

These wazzocks, who dare to rise above the parapet to proclaim unwise and unpopular opinions for no reason other than they think they should, are the most oppressed minority in the modern world. I have been one of their main oppressors and that's why I feel so guilty.

Which is why I am proposing making March 9th (International Women's Boxing Day, if you will) International Wazzocks' Day, a day set aside for all the

1 International Cat Day is August 8th.
2 World Toilet Day is on November 19th.

men who ask 'When's International Men's Day?' on International Women's Day. For that one day they are allowed to ask 'When's International Men's Day?' and no one is allowed to mock them, or call them stupid or point out that there is an International Men's Day and it's on November 19th.

In fact, on that day everyone has to search for their tweets and reply, 'Yeah, good point. There'd never be one, would there, due to political correctness gone mad. You're the only person who has ever noticed that. You're a genius.'

They won't appreciate it, though. They'll just reply, 'International Wazzocks' Day? When's International Non-Wazzocks' Day? There wouldn't be one because of political correctness towards wazzocks.'

Bad luck, I've already thought about that. It's March 10th. I knew they would say it, so I just made it the very next day. I'm always one step ahead of the wazzocks. I work out what the wazzocks will say and I come up with an answer. I'm ready for them. It's like a game of chess between me and the wazzocks. There are only two possible moves and I make sure I am one move ahead. It's pretty easy, because they just say the opposite of what you just said, so you can anticipate it.

So the wazzocks may come back at me and say, 'But when's International Non-Non-Wazzocks' Day?'

And I say, 'That's March 9th. That's a double negative. That's International Wazzocks' Day that you're describing. That's already covered.'

They say, 'Oh, I didn't know about double negatives.'
And I say, 'Yeah, that's why you're a wazzock.'
One step ahead of the wazzocks.

@▮▮▮▮▮ In all seriousness, when is international men's day?

> @Herring1967 Really? Seriously? It's November 19th

@▮▮▮▮▮ When is international Men's day?

> @Herring1967 November 19.
>
> > @▮▮▮▮▮ wait for real? I had no idea, thanks for the response.
> >
> > > @Herring1967 So few of them thank me. But that's what makes my job worthwhile.

@▮▮▮▮▮ But if there was an international men's day all hell would break loose . . .

> @Herring1967 Nope, Nov 19th and the dead and damned remain below.

@▮▮▮▮▮ Apparently International Mans Day was on 30th February, who knew?

> @Herring1967 No there isn't a 30th February. Your calendar is broken. It's actually November 19th.

@Herring1967 Just going to make myself a cup of tea – my wife is refusing to wait on me hand and foot for some reason – please try not to do any stupid tweets for five minutes

3

HOLD ON, YOU'RE A MAN![1] AREN'T YOU MAKING INTERNATIONAL WOMEN'S DAY ABOUT YOURSELF?

Damn, you've got me. There I was feeling smug about telling men not to steal focus from International Women's Day by making it all about themselves, while making the day all about myself: a man. Or close enough.

While many people have found what I am doing funny, there have always been some who think I do it for self-publicity or that I am stealing focus from International Women's Day by making it about me or that I am mocking the seriousness of the issues that International Men's Day highlights. Hey, look, I've got sympathy with some of this criticism. There's inarguably a paradox at the heart of it all.

'Stop mentioning International Men's Day on International

---

1 Thanks for noticing.

Women's Day,' says the man who spends all of March 8th doing nothing else.

When I began my Twitter odyssey (if only if had been on MySpace, then I could have called it my MySpace odyssey, which would have been a much better joke[1]), I had no idea it would become 'a thing'. I was just being mischievous and pedantic and trying to avoid work by messing around on social media.[2] I could never have imagined that some people would start looking forward to each year or say it was their favourite thing on International Women's Day or that it would provide column inches for lazy 'copy and paste' journalists or indeed become the subject of a short book that I would write during a global pandemic. I am not Nostradamus and I wish people would stop mistaking me for him.

Once it did start to become 'a thing', I could have discreetly withdrawn and stopped doing it. In a lot of ways, I'd have liked to stop doing it anyway, because it was really draining. But to begin with, at least, there were enough good reasons to carry on:

1. It was funny. Humour is of course subjective, but this was objectively extremely funny. And anyone who didn't find it funny just made it funnier. It's a joke that worked

---

1 Fuck you, Tom, for not inventing a more enduring platform.
2 Which is how I spend the vast majority of my working day. Writing is 1 per cent inspiration and 99 per cent prevarication.

on several levels but ultimately against myself. I was trapped in a web of my own making, every year mentally destroyed by my own hubris. And the longer it went on (on the whole) the funnier it was.

2. It was a test of my creativity. I had to try and make the answer to the same question funny over and over again. Not just for twenty-four hours, but for twenty-four hours every single year. Of course there was repetition – that was one of the main jokes – but even after nine years I was still finding new ways to express my surprise, my anger, my frustration.

3. The people asking 'When's International Men's Day?' were (predominantly) men. It seemed to me that it should be a man's job to deal with this irritant so that everyone else could get on with their day. If I could bat off the wasps with a newspaper then the rest of you could get on with enjoying the International Women's Day picnic. And if I failed they were still treated to the sight of a fat man running around, swiping at the air while being stung by angry insects.

4. I also knew that people who tweeted 'When's International Men's Day?' were doing it for the reaction. Some of them just wanted to raise a laugh, but others hoped for aggravation. Specifically they wanted to aggravate women. Which is why it was a good thing that I was a man. Women replying and chastising was exactly what they wanted. My guess was that for this type of pathetic

individual, the disrespect and mockery of a man would carry some weight.

I have no direct evidence that these guys wanted to infuriate and belittle women, beyond what has happened every time a woman has expressed an opinion online over the last two decades. So let's just call it a hunch.

I am not saying I didn't get any grief for my campaign, but an awful lot of the people I replied to said nothing at all or quietly deleted their question. Exactly like they wouldn't have done if I was a woman.

5. Another thing in my favour is that I have made a lot of tasteless, off-colour and offensive jokes myself. I am far from being a great example of a perfect man or political correctness. In my comedy career I have grown a Hitler moustache for a year to see what would happen to me; I have joked about murder, paedophilia, religion, politics, death and love, and made lots of jokes about women:

I am not a sexist. I've actually got a friend who's a woman, so I can't be sexist. I believe women should be treated as if they're equal.

Jerry Hall said that to keep their man, women should act 'like a cook in the kitchen, a maid in the parlour and a whore in the bedroom'. Better advice, ladies, if you want to keep your man, is to act like a whore in every room of the house.

As a kid I was obsessed with Germaine Greer's The Female Eunuch. *I never read it, but it had this brilliant cover: a naked torso of a woman with no arms, or legs or head . . . just the good bits. She might be a feminist but she knows how to get us guys going.*

Now, to some, such jokes show that I am a hypocrite or a charlatan. But what they demonstrate to me is that you can't accuse me of being some worthy, PC yoghurt-knitter on a high horse (except to those people who think showing any sign of empathy for another human being makes you a snowflake). Again I think this strengthens my hand when dealing with the kind of person who thinks there'd never be an International Men's Day because it wouldn't be allowed.[1]

6. Another aspect of my personality that makes me ideal for this role is my absolute bloody-minded persistence. I am like the Duracell Bunny of comedy, partly due to my obsessive nature and partly due to being like a dog with a bone. My life is littered with utterly pointless quests. I spent a couple of years in my mid-thirties attempting to spot the numbers 1–999 on UK number plates in numerical order (something I achieved in spite of those kind of number plates having been phased out years before);[2] I have a long-running podcast in which

1   They're wrong, by the way. There is one and it's on November 19th.
2   www.richardherring.com/cnps

I play myself at snooker in an attempt to find out who is best at the game, Me1 or Me2,[1] and over the last two years I have been attempting to clear all the stones off the field I walk my dog round and build a wall round the edge that can be visible from space. The fact that the field spans thirty-five acres and has several billion stones on it and I can only realistically move about fifty in a day is not stopping me.

For the International Women's Day marathon to work it's important that I attempt to get to every single person who has tweeted, even if they have incorrectly used the phrase National Man's Day or don't understand apostrophes and call it Mens' Day or Mans' Day. My dogged determination not to be defeated is what drives the whole thing. I am a man being sent gradually insane by the pointless and impossible task I have set myself. Some people have tried to help me out by creating bots that will answer the question for me, but not only does this not provide the masses with the tailored service I provide, but the bots are also unable to distinguish the ironic use of the question from the genuine. Nobody else has the right balance of madness, pomposity, determination, comedy chops, staying power and hubris to make this quest work. I am cursed, but it has to be ME.

7. Once I realised that people were prepared to sponsor me

---

1   They are both me.

and I could raise tens of thousands of pounds for charity for just twenty-four hours' work, it became very hard to walk away. Even if you are annoyed to distraction by me and don't find it funny, it's a special kind of person who can get infuriated by someone raising so much cash for victims of domestic abuse. Though, believe me, those very special kinds of people do exist.

Being able to turn stupidity into cold hard cash did make the whole thing a lot more palatable and less aggravating.

8. Most of all, though, targeting sexism is arduous and demanding and, let's face it, it takes a man to do a job like that.

@█████ Just a thought – when is International Men's Day . . . or did I miss it

> @Herring1967 Just a thought – think a bit before tweeting and google – or you might look like a buffoon. It's November 19th

@█████ I'm not being funny . . . but is there an international men's day?

> @Herring1967 You are not being funny. And there is. November 19th

@█████ Its time for men to have an international men's day and start a Men's too movement! We men need to make it a point to express all the extraordinary things we accomplish every day. Women do not appreciate our contributions to the world!

> @Herring1967 Neil,[1] you're full of good ideas. I have set one up for you. November 19th. Spread the word

When's international men's day? Do women get banned from the roads and boozers??

> @Herring1967 November 19th. And no, you've confused International men's day with the Handmaid's Tale

1 These tweets are real, but names have been changed to protect the ignorant.

@Herring1967 Having to put up with this relentless nonsense all the time? If only women knew what that was like.

4

WHY DO WE EVEN NEED AN INTERNATIONAL WOMEN'S DAY WHEN WOMEN ARE ALREADY EQUAL?

One of the more common reasons for opposition to a day to celebrate women is that we have already reached equality. And the arguments for that are solid:

- In the UK we've had TWO female Prime Ministers (out of fifty-five, but it's two out of the last seven which is practically 50/50)
- Sandi Toksvig presents *QI* now
- They don't even put the bare mammary glands of teenagers on Page 3 of *The Sun* any more
- There was that woman in the World Darts finals
- Some people claim women are unrepresented on UK coins and banknotes, but the queen is on every single one

and has been for bloody ages. And all the stamps. Also she is queen. And by the way that's one of eight queens of England and Britain in the last 1,200 years. And I haven't checked, but I reckon there were probably only eight kings in that time

- Harvey Weinstein is in prison, Jimmy Savile got his gravestone taken away and Prince Andrew can't show his face in Pizza Express

What more do women want? They don't want equality. They want dominance. They won't be happy until all men are kept in dungeons and their only function is to be milked for their gametes. And the terrible thing is that a lot of men are so in the thrall of the feminazis they would happily go along with that.

Of course, just for for balance, we also have to look at the arguments that equality is yet to be achieved. But those are a lot woollier:

- According to the Global Gender Gap Report carried out by the World Economic Forum in 2018[1], men and women are over a century away from gender parity and two centuries away from economic parity. That's only if things move at the pace they're going at the moment, though, so don't worry, there's every chance we could slow that down a bit.

---

1   http://www3.weforum.org/docs/WEF_GGGR_2018.pdf

- Only eight countries in the world give women the same legal working rights as men.[1] That's great news for all the women in Iceland, Belgium, Denmark, France, Latvia, Luxembourg, Sweden and Canada, which I think we can all agree is most of the world's countries.
- After the 2019 general election, only 34 per cent of MPs in the UK parliament were women. The global participation rate of women in national-level parliaments is around about 25 per cent. But that's because women famously only make up 25 per cent of the population. So, they're actually over-represented in the UK.
- If you're a woman then you're quite likely to be paying more for items like deodorant, socks, razors, shampoo and dry-cleaning,[2] even when the product is pretty much identical to the men's version. Men pay more for car insurance, though, but only because they're less likely to wear seat belts and more likely to be arrested for drink-driving. Which is extremely discriminatory of the insurance companies.
- As of 2018, women held 20.8 per cent of the board seats on Russell 1000 companies and it's more difficult for women lower down the ladder to even get promoted.

---

1 That's according to the World Bank's 'Women, Business and the Law Report' based on eight areas, including mobility, pay, marriage and pensions.
2 According to *Marie Claire* magazine, www.marieclaire.com/culture/a13816/things-that-cost-more-for-women

According to a report from McKinsey & Co.[1], for every hundred men promoted to the level of first-time manager, only seventy-two females are making that initial step.

- Women perform an estimated 2.6 times the amount of unpaid care and domestic work that men do, according to a survey by the United Nations[2]. The brilliant stand-up Catie Wilkins (I liked her so much that I married her) does a routine about how men weren't buying Diet Coke until they rebranded what was basically the same exact drink and called it Coke Zero. She wondered if men could be convinced to do other things they're not keen on and suggested rebranding hoovering as 'Mega Carpet Warfare'. I do at least 50 per cent of the housework so her tactic might be working. You should see my carpet – it's spotless.[3]

- 1.6 million women experienced domestic violence in the UK in the year ending March 2019[4] and eighty women were killed by their partners. Almost one in three women will experience domestic abuse in their

---

1 https://www.mckinsey.com/featured-insights/gender-equality/women-in-the-workplace-2018#

2 https://www.unwomen.org/en/news/in-focus/csw61/redistribute-unpaid-work

3 She also suggested renaming cunnilingus TURBO-TONGUE-HERO-AGAINST-THE-HOODED-AVENGER.

4 https://www.ons.gov.uk/peoplepopulationandcommunity/crimeandjustice/bulletins/domesticabuseinenglandandwalesoverview/november2019

lifetime[1], around 8 per cent of women experience domestic abuse each year. That's approaching double the amount of men who are victims of this crime[2]. Men are also less likely to have been repeat victims of domestic assault, less likely to be seriously injured or killed by a female partner and less likely to report feeling fearful in their own homes[3].

- Women are far more likely to be the victims of human trafficking[4]; to be illiterate due to lack of educational opportunities[5]; every year 12 million girls are married before the age of eighteen[6] and an estimated 200 million women have undergone female genital mutilation[7] ...

- It's all gone a bit serious and I haven't been able to make a flippant joke for ages, so let's end on a more light-hearted tone. A study from the University of Virginia showed that women are 47 per cent more likely to be severely

1 https://www.refuge.org.uk/our-work/forms-of-violence-and-abuse/domestic-violence/domestic-violence-the-facts/

2 https://www.ons.gov.uk/peoplepopulationandcommunity/crimeandjustice/articles/domesticabusefindingsfromthecrimesurveyforenglandandwales/yearendingmarch2017

3 https://www.womensaid.org.uk/information-support/what-is-domestic-abuse/domestic-abuse-is-a-gendered-crime/

4 https://www.un.org/sustainabledevelopment/blog/2016/12/report-majority-of-trafficking-victims-are-women-and-girls-one-third-children/

5 https://www.theguardian.com/global-development/2015/oct/20/two-thirds-of-worlds-illiterate-adults-are-women-report-finds

6 https://www.girlsnotbrides.org/about-child-marriage/

7 https://www.who.int/reproductivehealth/topics/fgm/prevalence/en/

injured in a car crash than men[1]. It's because car safety features, like head rests and preferred seating positions, have been designed for male drivers. Obviously the light-heartedness of this is relative, but I am doing my best with the material I am being provided with.

I could go on, but as you can see I am really scraping the bottom of the barrel trying to find examples of female inequality compared to all that has been achieved already. I am sure some feminists will be arguing things should go even further but to them I would say, what about the woman in the darts finals? Come on.

---

1   https://news.virginia.edu/content/
    royal-society-recognizes-uva-auto-crash-finding-statistic-year

@██████ When is International Men's Day? (Just asking for a friend.)

> @Herring1967 Can you get your friend to tweet too? Or can I trust you to pass on the info. At least give me his twitter handle so I can let him know. It's November 19th.

@████████ Is there an International Men's Day? #AskingForAFriend

> @Herring1967 So many good friends out there, searching for truth for their ignorant pals. Tell them it's November 19th and also inform them about google to save yourself time in the future

@██████ When exactly is International Men's Day??? Asking for a friend . . .

> @Herring1967 You don't have any friends. Or they'd have told you about November 19th. I can be your friend. Will you be my friend?

@██████ Is there an international men's day? Asking for a friend . . .

> @Herring1967 Another one? November 19th. Tell all your friends and ask them to tell their friends.

Or get people to ask themselves, rather than delegating this relatively simple task. I worry about these nervous friends too scared to ask basic questions.

@█████████ Is there an International Men's Day??? Asking for a friend

> @Herring1967 You have no friends. I checked. You are totally asking for yourself. It's November 19th. I don't have any friends either. Shall we team up? We could go metal detecting together.

@█████████ Is there an International Men's Day? Asking for a friend

> @Herring1967 Grab your friend by the balls, look into his eyes and tell him 'Yes, yes there is. It's November 19th and it's beautiful'. Why are you holding your own balls?

5

IF THERE'S STILL SO MUCH SEXISM, HOW COME I'VE NEVER EXPERIENCED IT?

If you're asking this question then I am going to astound you now with my psychic ability to determine your gender.

I am going to say that you're male.

Am I right?

If not, can you just double-check for me, because I'm pretty sure I got it right.

Let me try another one.

If you're white, then I am going to bet you haven't really had much experience of racism. Perhaps someone once called you a 'honky' or maybe you're confusing your life with an episode of *Starsky & Hutch*.

I'm a white man and I have never walked down the street and had someone shout out 'sugar tits' or mutter a racial epithet at me and I've walked down the street tens of thousands of times. So racism and sexism simply can't exist. That's just maths.

Though I have to say I am painfully aware of the prejudice against those who dare to love themselves. I can't go out of the house without someone calling me a 'wanker'. When will there be a day for us?[1]

Yeah, OK, I am a clever genius, making a brilliant point and I know there are a lot of men out there muttering about how they have experienced insults based on their appearance, or experienced intimidation and violence (most likely from other men, but let's not be churlish).

The problem is that our perception is clouded by reality. The world is so weighted towards white, middle-class men like myself that I have lived most of my life totally unaware of the access I have to all kinds of power-ups and secret keys that others don't share. That example of car safety being designed with men in mind and being dangerous for female drivers and passengers is a perfect example of the invisible nature of sexism in society.

Deborah Frances-White, the British–Australian host of the highly recommended podcast phenomenon *The Guilty Feminist*, explained this brilliantly when appearing on my podcast. With my tongue slightly in my cheek I suggested

---

1 National Masturbation Day is May 7th, but International Masturbation Day is May 28th and the whole month of May is set aside to celebrate the greatest love of all. Hopefully soon it will become the year long festival that it deserves to be (and is).

that the playing field was surely basically level for men and women now. Her reply was:

When I first came to London I got a job as a nanny. I'd driven in Sydney, but I'd never driven in London before and everyone said, 'Driving in London is so scary … you've got to be really aggressive, you've got to get out there … No one's going to wait for you. You've gotta be assertive.'

… But I found this was a stereotype about Londoners. They weren't impolite drivers at all. They always let you in. They were lovely.

Then about six months later I got a boyfriend and I drove his car one day and I couldn't get out and I ended up being backed up into a cul de sac.

I was like, 'What's going on?'

And he said, 'You can't drive this car the way you drive the Land Rover, like a tank down the middle of the road and everyone gets out of your way. This is a VW Golf. No one's going to get out of your way.'

I said, 'I don't drive the Land Rover like a tank.'

And he said, 'Yes, you do.'

And I was like, 'Oh. I thought everyone was polite. Turns out that I'm an arsehole.'

That's the same for six-foot-four men called Toby with pinkie rings. They don't know they're an arsehole, they think you're polite.

All they've ever driven is a tank, so everyone gets out of their way, so they don't know what it's like to drive a VW Golf.

If you think there's no longer sexism then you just need to ask women about it. Ask a few. Probably ones you know rather than random ones in the street. You will find that most of them have so many stories of harassment, of being passed over at work and having their ideas ignored, or worse, ignored and then repeated by a man who takes credit for them. All those things will have happened to men too, perhaps, but overall not to the same degree, not with the same frequency, not with the same level of peril. And if you ask a man, I bet you the stories won't trip off the tongue quite as readily, even if they eventually manage to think of an example.

Another person who really brought home my unseen privilege is black comedian Nathan Caton. He tweeted,

> To anyone who says 'racial prejudice is an American issue. We don't have anything like that in the UK' . . . I thought I'd try this. How many fingers would you have left? #blacklivesmatter #blackouttuesday #racism

There was a link to a video where you were asked to hold up ten fingers and put a finger down for every scenario that you had encountered.[1] There were around a dozen of them, including:

- Put a finger down if you have been called a racial slur
- Put a finger down if you've been followed in a store unnecessarily
- Put a finger down if someone has crossed the street to avoid passing you
- Put a finger down if you have been stopped or detained by police for no valid reason

By the end of the video Nathan had run out of fingers. I still had ten fingers (maybe nine and a half) sticking up. This is a man who does the exact same job as me and yet our life experience is so different.

I wonder what that's about . . .

Oh.

Ohhhhhh.

---

1   See it here: https://twitter.com/NathanCaton/status/1268201190162149376, or, if it's easier, google 'Nathan Caton Twitter Finger'.

@████ How about an International Men's Day!? No? Okay. : /

> @Herring1967 Yes Yes. Let's you and me set it up
>
> @Herring1967 We could take off our shirts and drink beer and mend a car. You in?
>
> @Herring1967 Then maybe at end we could wrestle each other. Just manfully. You in?
>
> @Herring1967 Please respond. About the Int men's day idea. Is Nov 19 good for you?
>
> @Herring1967 Hello?

@████ When is International Men's Day? Oh and is there a bigger cuck faggot than Richard Herring on earth?

> @Herring1967 It's November 19th. And yes, there must be. I just like answering general knowledge questions. I am not a very good cook. I once kissed a man in college but it wasn't really for me.

@████ Is that guy going to do that thing about those tweets about 'international men's day?'

> @Herring1967 Surely he won't need to. Not after all these years. Everyone must know by now, right?

@▮▮▮▮▮▮▮▮ Boring libtard 'comedian' @Herring1967 been telling the same joke all morning for no apparent reason.

| @Herring1967 You're the reason

6

WHAT IF SOCIETY IS ACTUALLY SEXIST AGAINST MEN?

Every International Women's Day, a man who works in your office will say, 'I agree that society is sexist – it's sexist against men.' And then he'll pull a face that suggests he has just made the greatest satirical point of all time and that you would never have even thought of that and your mind is blown.

But what if that man is right?

Have I blown your mind? Because I am pulling a face like I have.[1]

What if feminists have duped us all and in fact it's actually *men* who have drawn the short straw in terms of equality.

You might ask how women have managed to skew things

---

1   Email me at herring1967@gmail.com and I will send you a picture of me pulling the face. Please include the subject heading, 'I would like a picture of Richard Herring pulling a face like he has blown my mind.'

so heavily in their favour in spite of their poor representation in positions of power or the media. You have to conclude that it's some kind of evil witch magic. We'd better start burning them just in case.

All right. I'm getting ahead of myself. Let's look at the facts fairly and impartially before we leap to burning anyone. And we should at least start with dunking, so they have a chance to prove they aren't witches.[1]

Of course, it's hard for me to be unbiased because I am a man. It would really suit me if I could blame my failures to get as far in life as I'd like to[2] and to achieve the things my mum said I was capable of[3] on institutionalised prejudice against me because of my penis.[4]

But I will do my best to remain open minded before concluding that this is obviously all women's fault.

While it's true that the men with power and wealth have advantages that few women enjoy, there are still many men who are disadvantaged by a system that nevertheless they are prepared to fight and die for/defend vociferously on Twitter (delete as applicable).

That's one of the major disadvantages, right? Not the Twitter one, the one about being prepared to fight and die. Because that dying in war thing, while not exclusively a

---

1 It's OK. They are. Be patient. You'll get your burning.
2 God-King of the Universe.
3 Being the best at everything and the handsomest boy in the world.
4 Which eight out of ten people who have seen it describe as 'adequate', so ignore anything else you might have heard about it.

male privilege, has been something men have been doing for centuries. Sure, civilian women may also be killed in the crossfire (and be the victims of sexual assault, bombings and lack of access to lifesaving medical care) but the vast majority of the people doing the fighting (and the killing and raping, but that's for another day) are men. Men are encouraged to see death in battle as a manly, honourable, even divine end, and also to ignore the fact that the people sending them to the front are often quite well hidden in protective bunkers, miles away from the fighting, drinking fine wine and being waited upon by snooty butlers.

Men's rights activists are keen to point out this male disposability, which sees us (and by 'us' I very much mean not me) sent down mines and taking on the most dangerous of jobs, even in peace time. Men are more likely to get cancer than women (who have an extra copy of some protective genes in their DNA – I told you they were witches), more likely to be homeless and more likely to die young.

Men are given over 60 per cent more prison time than women for the same offence and women are significantly more likely to avoid charges and conviction all together[1]. Rape in prison is another undiscussed problem for men (once again, nearly all the rapists are men, but it's really not fair to keep bringing that up), and one that is generally treated as a joke; how many times have you seen some variant on

---

1   According to University of Michigan Law and Economics Research Paper, No. 12–018.

dropping the soap in the showers played for laughs? Men are also disadvantaged when it comes to who gets custody of the children in divorce settlements and not getting equal paternity leave. In the Western world, boys are more likely to drop out of school and less likely to get a degree.

Boys are still discouraged from discussing their feelings and emotions and in most countries men are three or four times more likely to die by suicide. Even though more women suffer from depression and are more likely to attempt to kill themselves, men die more often because they generally choose more violent methods.

This last statistic is not only depressing and horrifying, but it also shows how redundant and offensive it is to turn any of these issues into a competition. The headline here is that people are killing themselves and we should be doing more to stop it happening to anyone, regardless of gender. If gender is relevant then we should of course look into why,[1] but you either think suicide is something we should try and prevent or you don't (I am hoping it's the former).

If you care about domestic abuse, sexual assault, depression and education then don't start a fight with someone who also cares about those things. If you want equality, you don't argue with someone who wants equality too. You want the same thing, you wazzock. If women achieve equality, then men do as well.

---

1 Something that the charity CALM is at the forefront of: www.thecalmzone.net

It's fair enough that for twenty-four hours International Women's Day puts emphasis on helping women. There are 364 other days (365 in a leap year) on which to address how it all affects men. If you're really interested in the issues mentioned above then why aren't you getting behind World Mental Health Day (October 10th) or World Suicide Prevention Day (September 10th) or International Day of Education (January 24th) or World Homeless Day (also October 10th)? Or how about fucking International Men's Day?[1] (Not sure of the date of that one, but will google it next March 8th and forget to make a note of it like everyone else.) There's just one day of the year when it's counterproductive to make any of these points.

If it was International Men's Day and you were making a valid comment about the need to look into the causes of why so many men kill themselves and a woman piped up and said, 'Actually more women *attempt* suicide then men, so it's actually a female problem,' you would have a right to feel like they were trying to disrupt and annoy you and that their real motive wasn't concern about suicide.

But women don't do this on International Men's Day. If anyone is tweeting 'When's International Women's Day?' on November 19th, it is almost certainly a sarcastic response to what happens on March 8th. I can sift the ironic comment

---

1 NB: I am using 'fucking' for emphasis there. There is as yet no Fucking International Men's Day, but if anyone starts one up I will do my best to promote it.

from the genuine one with about 98 per cent accuracy — believe me, I've had a lot of practice. This is why I've said no bot can ever take my 'When's International Men's Day?' job.

Men have a point. The system we have can treat men extremely badly. Ironically, the patriarchy is really not a good thing for possibly the majority of men, and yet the majority of men will still support it and defend it and moan about feminists trying to ruin everything.

But who is it who is sending you to war and to prison? Who is running the system where boys flunk out of school? Who is telling you to conform to masculine stereotypes and to man up because boys don't cry?

It's the guys in the bunker with the butlers; the ones who take cocaine and don't get sent to prison; who grab women by the pussy, admit it and still keep their jobs; who send their kids to private school so they don't flunk out; who only give jobs to other men like themselves.

The patriarchy is grabbing you by the pussy and you're such a little bitch you actually cheerlead for it.

When are you going to grow some balls and become a feminist?

@▮▮▮▮ I want international mens day so I can post pictures of my junk. Without being banned by twitter and being arrested by the police.

> @Herring1967 There is one on November 19th, but to be fair it isn't a purge day for perverts, so you might want to angle for a specific day for that

@▮▮▮▮ Where's the International men's day? #InternationalWomensDay

> @Herring1967 It is in the future, it is in the past. It is on the planet earth. It's on November 19th. Hope you will join in.

@▮▮▮▮ I can't wait for International men's day . . . oh wait

> @Herring1967 Yeah you'll have to wait but only 8 months. It's all down to the linear nature of time.

@▮▮▮▮ How Strange it is ,There is no Man's Day . Although a Man too deserves a Day !! your opinions Please ! #HappyWomensDay2020

> @Herring1967 My opinion is that they do deserve it and that's why there is one on November 19th

@█████ Is is politically correct for men to feel left out?
No International Men's Day.

> @Herring1967 Not politically incorrect. Just ignorant of facts. There's one on November 19th. Enjoy it.

7

IS FEMALE EQUALITY REALLY THE SAME AS MALE EQUALITY?

Yes.

@█████████ can we do international men's day too? Shit wld seriously shit down

> @Herring1967 Noticed no shit shitting down last Nov 19. maybe next.

@████████ time we start men empowerment but equally treat men and women.Y no International MENS dAY?

> | @Herring1967 Apart from ON nOVEMBER 19TH

@██████████ Just googled International mens day and couldn't find anything. Seems about right. #InternationalWomensDay

> | @Herring1967 Really?

@████████ I only asked a fucking question

> | @Herring1967 I only gave you the fucking answer. Why so angry?

@█████████ When is International Mens Day, or are we done with all the equality ballshit now or something?

> | @Herring1967 Nov 19. Hold on, ballshit?

@██████ Men relax yourself's international men's day is November 17th

  | @Herring1967 Um . . .

8

CAN A MAN REALLY BE A FEMINIST?

Well, now you've opened a can of worms.

If I hadn't bothered to google it I'd have said 'sure'. I've got a T-shirt saying, THIS IS WHAT A FEMINIST LOOKS LIKE. Surely a T-shirt wouldn't lie?[1]

But if I've learned one thing in the past nine years, it's to always google things before talking about them in public.

Whether men can be feminists is another issue that seems to unite hard-line feminists and men's rights activists, both of whom wholeheartedly say NO. These groups always *say* they disagree with each other, but then they think alike so often. Is it me or do you think they might be into each other?

So what have men got against being feminists?

Given that so many males are obsessed with the idea of

---

1 Theresa May had one too and she's a woman, so it must make me a great feminist. QED.

equality (on International Women's Day, at least), it's odd that they wouldn't support a cause that is aiming for exactly that. Either they don't *really* care about equality, or they are put off by the name.

I suspect they're thinking: *If it's about being equal, why does it have 'fem' at the start? Does that make me appear effeminate if I support it? Do words have the power to actually alter the way that my gender is perceived? Feminism isn't about equality, it's about women getting the upper hand.*

I'd suggest renaming the movement 'Egalatrianism', but I expect those men still wouldn't get involved because it has the word 'gal' in it.

Others are doubtless put off by the stereotype of feminists as ball-breaking, boiler-suited men-haters who think they're all rapists and want to send them to prison for patting someone on the bum thirty years ago, or destroy their career with an unfounded (or well-founded) rumour. It's hard to support something that makes you feel like the enemy.

Many men are suspicious of men who call themselves feminists. White, American comedian Bill Burr said in his 2019 Netflix stand-up special *Paper Tiger*:[1]

> We now have the male feminist. Where the fuck did that come from? . . . You can't do it. You're a man! You can agree with it, you can empathise with it, you can do all of that

---

1   The fact that it's part of a comedy routine might mean we shouldn't take this at 100 per cent face value.

shit. But you can't be it any more than I can stand here and be like, 'I'm a Black Panther. Fight the Power.' Then I walk out the door a blue-eyed white dude and I get to live that fucking life.

He puts voice to what I suspect many men believe, namely that being a male feminist is just a way to try 'and get some pussy', comparing them to sixteen-year-old boys on their first date with a girl, thinking, 'Just agree with her. Maybe she'll touch it.'

Many feminists would also argue that they don't want men in their ranks. In 2008, Cath Elliott asked in the *Guardian*:

Can everyone who supports the idea of women's rights call themselves a feminist, or are there other criteria that have to be met before people are allowed to sport the label? Like having a vagina, for example,[1] or having experience of life as a female and all the attendant discriminations that that brings? Can men ever really be feminists, or should pro-feminist be consigned to the sidelines, welcome allies in the struggle for gender equality, but disqualified from full membership by dint of their unasked-for but nonetheless privileged position as fully paid-up members of the male fraternity?

---

1 And hasn't that definition become a lot more contentious for feminists in the last decade.

Those guys trying to use feminism to pull are really alienating everyone, right?

The word 'feminism'[1] covers a lot of different viewpoints and conflicting ideologies, but if it's about searching for political, personal and social equality then surely men have a part to play – even if it is just to accept there are privileges they need to relinquish and behaviour they need to address in themselves and chastise in others.

I think most women would welcome male feminists, but to try and keep everyone happy, perhaps they should be given a rebrand (in the same way that Catie Wilkins made housework and cunnilingus man-friendly). What about 'Equalisers'? Then men could pretend they were Edward Woodward, shooting down unfairness whenever it raises its ugly head.

In the end, it doesn't really matter what you call yourself. Men's participation and support is required to achieve equality, and equality will benefit nearly everyone. In some ways, men actually need to overthrow the patriarchy more urgently than women do. Masculinity is in a crisis of its own making, and toxic masculinity and ludicrous overconfidence in our own ability is harming men, too.

To illustrate that, let's ask another question that was a talking point on social media in 2019 . . .

---

1 Coined by a man, incidentally – Charles Fourier. You're welcome, girls.

@████ Is there an International Men's Day? If not we need a Congressional resolution condemning this!

> @Herring1967 Possibly find out if there is one first before planning how you're going to react if there isn't. Just a little pause. A send in the middle of the tweet. You'll probably get an answer and then not have to come up with a solution to your imagined injustice. It's November 19

@████ Where's international men's day huh oh wait feminism is the true definition of unequal

> @Herring1967 Again it's really worth waiting for an answer to a question before you carry on with your answer. It's November 19th. And now you look like a proper ninny whose excellent point about feminism has been undermined.

@████ When's international mens day then?! Of course there isn't one. So much for equality!!

> @Herring1967 Woah Woah. After asking a question, it makes sense to await an answer, lest you stumble onwards and make a jackass of yourself. Press send after the question mark. It's

November 19th. Hopefully you won't answer your own questions like this again.

@■■■■■■ Really when is international men's day ?!! Come on I want to know .

> @Herring1967 Sorry, I've got to you as quickly as possible. Seems rude to be that impatient before you'd even sent the tweet though. Realistically no one could answer it before you'd hit send. I'll let it pass cos I can see you are passionate about the day – November 19th

@■■■■■■ Can't wait to celebrate International Men's Day by . . . Oh there isn't one. Big surprise.

> @Herring1967 This is going to be so embarrassing for you. There IS one. On November 19th. I admire your confidence, but combined with ignorance that's a dangerous weapon.

9

COULD I WIN A POINT IF I PLAYED SERENA WILLIAMS AT TENNIS?

Unless you are a professional tennis player (or an exceptionally good amateur of county level or above), the answer to this one is almost certainly, 'No fucking way, you deluded shit-pipe. How dare you even entertain the idea?'

But according to a YouGov poll, 12 per cent of British men who were asked, 'Do you think if you were playing your very best tennis, you could win a point off Serena Williams?' answered in the affirmative.

One in eight men think they could nick a point off the player who has won more Grand Slams in the Open Era than any other person (including one when she was eight weeks pregnant). Only if they were playing their very best tennis, though – they're not insane.

You almost have to admire the confidence. You know, if it wasn't so utterly, thoughtlessly ridiculous.

A further 14 per cent of men said they 'didn't know' if they could do it. Which implies they think it's a possibility. Maybe they had to answer 'don't know' because they were unaware of who Serena Williams is, or because they'd never played tennis so weren't sure how good they'd be at it. Or maybe they'd just lost their fucking minds like the 12 per cent who thought they definitely could.

That's one in four men who think they definitely could or at least might possibly be able to win a point against Serena Williams. And not one in four men in their twenties who regularly exercise. One in four men including people like me, Christopher Biggins, the bloke who played Mr Muscle in those adverts and Prince Philip. I wonder which one of us would win a point. That's four men. Maths says one of us probably can.

Have one in four men even picked up a tennis racquet in the last ten years? Have one in four men *ever* played tennis at any level? I'm including Swingball.

I suspect that most of them are thinking: 'Hey, in a tennis match any player is bound to serve a double fault or hit a ball a bit too long occasionally. That's where I'd pick up a point. I am not mental.' Sure, that happens quite often in the two- to three-hour matches Serena plays against professional tennis players.

But if she's playing me or the bloke who played Mr Muscle,

I reckon she could probably take her serve down from its 126 miles per hour maximum speed to maybe 68 miles per hour and I still wouldn't even see it as it whizzed past my head – or (if I'd been showing off before the match about how I could win a point) repeatedly and violently into my testicles. You'd have to ask the bloke who played Mr Muscle to find out if he thought he'd do any better.

I don't think she'd be very likely to double fault. Even if she somehow contrived to make one single fault in the forty-eight points it would take her to beat me by two sets to love, it would only be because she'd been hit on the head with an anvil that had fallen from a passing helicopter. And maybe not even then. It wouldn't be advisable to rely on that eventuality. It would look suspicious now I've written about it, anyway. Especially if anyone checked my Amazon order history. There are many reasons I could have bought that anvil, though.

Oh, but what if I got my racquet to one of her twenty-four serves and by luck it pinged off into a part of the court she couldn't get to? That would probably work if she forgot how to move her legs.

Luckily for her it would never happen. I wouldn't get a touch.

If you don't believe me, check out the video made by @Itsblackculture on Twitter. It shows Serena hitting some (by her standards) pretty tame serves to three fairly fit young men, who clearly believed they had a chance of returning them.

They do not do well.

They swing wildly at nothing when the ball has already passed them. One of them is told he is making men look bad and he whines, 'I know. She put some spin on it and it went further out here than I was ready for.'

All three men line up to cover half the court in the hope of getting a return, but Serena still leaves them flailing and dumbfounded. There is one moment of triumph when one declares, 'I got a snick on it.' I think he might have just hit the ground.

Another fellow goes down like he's been hit by a sniper when one of these gentle serves hits him in the leg. And that's not surprising, is it? It's going at maybe 50 mph. Like a snail compared to her regular serves, but like a rocket ship compared to yours.

I firmly believe that even with one hand tied behind her back, Serena could beat 99 per cent of people on the planet. If you blindfolded her and spun her round a few times then maybe it would go down to 98.

So, are 12 per cent of men overestimating their own abilities or underestimating Serena's? Or are they just assuming that because they are a man they'd be capable of providing serious competition for a woman, even if that woman is Serena Williams? It would be interesting to know if they thought they could take a point off Rafael Nadal or Andy Murray, but alas they weren't asked about that.

Only 3 per cent of women thought they could win a point

(with a still fairly high 10 per cent claiming not to know). But that's one in thirty-three, as opposed to one in eight, showing there are significantly fewer deluded women.

Without knowing why these men thought they could triumph against Serena and whether they thought they could beat Nadal, it's hard to come to any firm conclusions. And just like with International Men's Day, it's fun to take the piss out of men with little self- (or general) awareness.

This kind of insane overconfidence is often thought to give men an advantage when it comes to applying for jobs, because men are more likely to overestimate their abilities and women to underestimate theirs.

But the answer to this problem is not to encourage women to become as comically overconfident as men. We want fewer idiots in the world, not more. Perhaps we need to encourage men to accept who they are and which skills they have and which they should delegate.

If businesses (and countries) are run by men with an overinflated idea of their own abilities and who refuse to acknowledge their limitations, or the strengths of others, there can be serious consequences for us all.

@█████ When is international men's day?

> @Herring1967 Claire. It's November 19th. But don't side with men. They don't respect you for it. They laugh at you when you're not there.

@█████ When is it international mens day? #InternationalWomensDay #IWD2020

> @Herring1967 When's international apostrophe day?[1] Am I right? Only kidding, Tracy. International Men's Day is 19th November

@█████ So when are we acknowledging International Men's Day?

> @Herring1967 Today it seems

@█████ So, when is International Men's Day? I raised four sons and have five grandsons. Strong masculinity needs to be celebrated also!

> @Herring1967 November 19th. Even for the weak ones who want to cry.

@Herring1967 The tweets from the women make my heart hurt.

1 It's August 16th.

10

WHAT'S WRONG WITH BEING CONFIDENT?

I am living proof that overconfidence can work out.

I don't know what possessed the twenty-one-year-old me to believe he was funny enough to stand on stage in front of paying, properly grown-up strangers and try to make them laugh. Or what prompted him to carry on trying even when he regularly failed to do so.

Whether it was self-belief or just wanting it so much that I wouldn't give up (or simply luck or privilege), it somehow panned out OK. Though, to be fair, many people still consider me deluded.

Overreaching is of course a great way to find out if you have what it takes (or might one day) and it tends to be something that men are encouraged to do. But if a woman does the same then she is often seen as pushy. We have generally taught our daughters to be modest and to think of others before themselves, and while we *say* that sort of stuff to our sons, we laugh when they ignore us, and slap them on the back.

As we've seen with Serena, male self-belief can defy reality and become embarrassing. We've all seen hideous examples of mansplaining on social media, including men correcting female authors on the motivations of the characters they have written about,[1] a man telling Anindita Debnath Nair how to pronounce her own name[2] or, most gloriously, a man incorrectly trying to explain what a vagina is and then doubling and tripling down when challenged by Dr Jennifer Gunter, an international expert on the vagina and vulva.[3]

This desire to be seen as omnipotent and macho would only be funny, if it didn't have devastating and sometimes deadly effects for others and even the men themselves.

I am writing this book in the midst of the lockdown due to Covid-19, or what I am calling 'The First Great Lockdown'[4]. It's fair to say that not everyone has been taking isolation as seriously as they should be (if you know a better way to test your eyesight than driving thirty miles with your family in

---

1 Gail Simone coped with this with impressive reserve and wit: www.thepoke.co.uk/2019/03/06/mansplained-comic-writer-takedown-brutal

2 Shit, just realised I am going to have to pronounce that for the audiobook. No need to check it, though. I reckon I probably know.

3 It's worth reading the whole encounter: www.iflscience.com/health-and-medicine/man-tries-to-explain-what-a-vagina-is-to-a-gynaecologist-it-does-not-go-well

4 You may be reading this during the second one

the car, then please tell me), but men are more likely to take risks with the virus. According to a report from Middlesex University,[1] men were less likely to wear a face mask than women, which can be 'partly explained by the fact that men more than women believe that they will be relatively unaffected by the disease'.

In fact, men are more vulnerable to it. The report continues, 'Men more than women agree that wearing a face covering is shameful, not cool, a sign of weakness, and a stigma', all of which makes them less likely to wear a mask.

Men are so desperate to conform to society's ideals of masculinity and not be shown to possess fear that they are willing to risk their lives (and, more crucially, your life) to conform. This goes right to the top. Our leaders' responses to the crisis have made the difference between life and death, possibly for thousands of people.

The state leaders who are treating Covid-19 like an enemy in a war and demonstrating their machismo by refusing to wear face masks or change their behaviour are generally the ones (as I write) who are leading the nations with the highest rates of infection and death.[2] The countries who have followed the science and acted quickly to get into lockdown, where the state leaders have realised it isn't actually possible to go to war with a virus without nuking yourself, have flattened the curve much more quickly. I am not the only

1   https://psyarxiv.com/tg7vz
2   Notably the UK, USA and Brazil.

one to notice that many of these countries are led by women. New Zealand, Germany, Iceland, Finland, Norway, Taiwan, Denmark are – at the time of writing – led by rational female leaders, all of whom, I'd bet, have a realistic idea of how likely they are to win a point off Serena Williams, but who have also managed to control the spread of a pandemic much more effectively than their male counterparts.

As the *Guardian* commented: 'Plenty of countries with male leaders – Vietnam, the Czech Republic, Greece, Australia – have also done well. But few with female leaders have done badly.'

It's perfectly possible for men to lead in the way that these women have, but it's interesting that so many male leaders see their job as a (sometimes literal) dick-swinging contest and that their dicks are (not so literally) scythes that can mow down the very people who voted for them.

This is a problem with our perception of what a man should be and it's a problem that goes to the core of the crisis that masculinity faces.

Overconfidence might get you into a big job and if you're lucky nothing disastrous will happen and you'll manage to wing it so it looks like you know what you're doing. But if you get put to the test then it could be embarrassing for you and disastrous for everyone else.

When I compare the leadership of Boris Johnson with someone like New Zealand's Jacinda Ardern, I start wishing that I lived on the other side of the world. It feels like Ardern is trying to move the human race forwards, while Johnson is pushing us back to a past that is no longer relevant.

Ardern herself says: 'One of the criticisms I've faced over the years is that I'm not aggressive enough or assertive enough, or maybe somehow, because I'm empathetic, I'm weak. I totally rebel against that. I refuse to believe that you cannot be both compassionate and strong.'

@█████ Hey Richard. I'd love to cave your face in with a shovel. Happy IWD

> @Herring1967 If this happens, this guy might be prime suspect.
>
> @Herring1967 That's one of the foolish mistakes that many shovel-based assailants make, revealing their plan. Plus using a shovel as a weapon.
>
> @Herring1967 But if it takes my shovel-based martyrdom to truly educate the world about international men's day then so be it.
>
> @Herring1967 Plus, you know, if I see a bloke approaching me with a shovel now I will probably treat him with caution
>
> @Herring1967 Mind you, he has just given the perfect excuse for someone else to cave my face in with a shovel and let him take the rap.

11

WHERE'S OUR GOOGLE DOODLE?

Not many people bother to reply when I answer their tweet and tell them when International Men's Day is,[1] but those who do will sometimes say something along the lines of, 'Oh, I didn't know about that. Maybe because nobody makes a big deal of it, like they do on International Women's Day.'

Obviously, that's a little bit hurtful to me, given what a big deal I have been making of International Men's Day for ALMOST A DECADE. But I try to be the bigger person and let it slide.

Once men realise there *is* an International Men's Day,[2] rather than feeling happy with that and getting on with celebrating it, they prefer to complain that it isn't taken as

---

1   It's November 19th.
2   It's on November 19th.

seriously as International Women's Day. Some of their reasons come off as a bit desperate, though.

In 2020 I noticed quite a few men informing me that although I was right, there is an International Men's Day,[1] it is not officially recognised by the UN. They appeared very hurt by this. I imagined some of them were on the point of tears. What's the point in having a day if the UN doesn't recognise it?

To be fair, the UN does seem to be mocking men, because it has instead declared November 19th to be World Toilet Day. That's some high-grade trolling. You'd rather celebrate toilets than men, would you, UN? You think toilets are better than men? Is this some sly dig at us for leaving the toilet seat up? Or for pissing on it and the floor when we're a bit drunk or tired, and then not bothering to clean it up? Why are men the ones who are expected to move the toilet seat, anyway? It's the women who need it down, not us. Unless we're doing a poo. But statistically that's probably only about one in six times we use it, so I'd still say women should move it if they're that bothered. How about we'll move it up, they can move it down? Do they even want equality?

To be fair, World Toilet Day is pretty important as it aims to tackle the global sanitation crisis. Over 4 billion people in the world live without safely managed toilet facilities, which leads to 432,000 people dying every year as a result

---

1 On November 19th.

of diarrheal diseases.[1] So maybe toilets do deserve their day[2] (though we had dibs on November 19th first – couldn't they have taken another date?), but a quick look at the UN website shows they have days for some right trivial rubbish:

- February 10th: World Pulses Day – a day dedicated to beans, lentils and peas. Are leguminous vegetables more important than men?
- June 3rd: World Bicycle Day. Bicycles don't deserve a day. At least lump them in with toilets and chairs and have a World Things You Sit On Day.
- June 21st: International Day of Yoga. I know some men do yoga, but it's mainly for women, isn't it? What about men? When's International Nunchucks Day?
- June 27th: Micro-, Small and Medium-sized Enterprises Day. Are you taking the piss now, UN?
- November 21st: World Television Day. Hey! Every day is World Television Day.

Look, it stings that there's a day for bicycles and not men, but let's step back and think about this. When has anyone ever cared about the UN's opinion on anything? Do men get to November 19th, intent on making a big fuss, and then read that, once again, the UN has failed to officially recognise their day, and so they take down their bunting,

---

1   www.un.org/en/events/toiletday
2   But when will it be World Bidet Day?

cancel the parade and go back to bed? I certainly find it very hard to celebrate my birthday each year, knowing that the UN doesn't give a flying fuck about it. Not even a card from Boutros Boutros-Ghali.[1]

Personally, I am glad the UN doesn't recognise International Men's Day. It makes the day look a bit more underground and dangerous. Who did you like best at school? The officially recognised swotty prefects or the kids who hung around by the bike shed smoking weed? Cool things getting official recognition always ruins them. Look at Jesus. Subversive and edgy when only twelve really dedicated blokes liked Him, but now your gran and even Donald Trump are into Him. Lame!

Do you really want Man's Day recognised by The Man?

I agree, in some ways it would be nice if the UN took men as seriously as it does lentils, so maybe it's not totally unreasonable to point out the disparity.

An altogether more pathetic – though surprisingly common – complaint is that International Men's Day isn't treated equally because it doesn't get a Google Doodle[2] like the women's one sometimes does. How unfair can you get? How can women complain about human trafficking when

---

1 I suppose he thinks that dying in 2016 lets him off the hook, but I am still taking it personally.
2 For those who still haven't worked out how to use the most visited website in the world, the Google Doodle is the fun way that the popular search engine adapts its logo on its home page to celebrate anniversaries, holidays and notable people.

they get a cartoon of Emmeline Pankhurst to look at on their day, whereas men just have a regular search bar or an animation celebrating toilets?

It's so hard being a man. We don't get a Google Doodle. Where's our Google Doodle? We want our Google Doodle because we are MEN!

If you are holding up UN recognition and Google Doodles as proof of how the world is weighted against you, then maybe you should put this book down, go downstairs and say to your mum, 'Look, I'm forty-five years old now. I think it's time for me to move out and find my own place and maybe in a year or two, when I have settled down and got a job, you can stop paying me pocket money. ... Also, I hate to say it, but you have to stop breast-feeding me. At least in public.'

I am saying that you are a baby.

And yes, there is a day for you. It's Baby Day and it's on May 2nd.

And I have some bad news for you about that, too (please don't throw your toys out of the pram)... It's not recognised by the UN. And as far as I can tell it has never had a Google Doodle.

@████████ Today is literally International Woman's Day but when is International Men's Day? And, more importantly, when is International Hedgehog Day?

| @Herring1967 November 19th and February 2nd

@████████ So when is international transsexual day!?

| @Herring1967 Transgender days on 31st March, 20th Nov or choose as you self-identify

@████████ intergalactic humans day, when's that then smart ass?

| @Herring1967 Plnagtrak the 7034th

12

IS THERE ANYTHING THAT DOESN'T HAVE A DAY?

One thing that you may have gleaned from this book is that there actually *is* an International Men's Day and it's on November 19th (please try to remember this, there will be a test at the end). A second thing you might have noticed is that there are an awful lot of national, international and world days. It's almost like having a day dedicated to something is not really that important or original an accolade. Because if there's an Ice Cream For Breakfast Day,[1] then maybe a day celebrating men isn't all that big an achievement.

Pretty much every day in the calendar is set aside to promote one or sometimes three or four causes. Even February 29th has Rare Disease Day, which would be a neat little joke,

---

1   First Saturday in February.

but they cheat and have it on February 28th on non-leap years, the monsters.

It's actually pretty difficult to think of something that doesn't have a day. If you don't believe me check out the page 'List of minor secular observances' on Wikipedia.[1]

Feb 5th: World Nutella Day.[2] Every year, like an Italian Willy Wonka, Ian Ferrero (the inventor of Nutella[3]) chooses one Nutella fan to lead the celebration of the cocoa and hazelnut spread. But when's World Marmite Day?[4]

March 10th: Mario Day. That's a day for Mario from the Super Mario Bros. But when will there be a Luigi Day?[5]

June 28th: CAPS LOCK DAY. YES, THERE'S A DAY FOR PEOPLE WHO WRITE EVERYTHING WITH THE CAPS LOCKS ON AND SO LOOK LIKE SHOUTING LOONS IN EVERY INTERNET EXCHANGE.[6]

July 2nd: World UFO Day. There's a day for little green men, but when will there be a day for little green women?

---

1 And if you're thinking that Wikipedia deserves a day, you're in luck – it's January 15th.
2 https://nationaltoday.com/world-nutella-day – it's worth checking this site out if you are unclear about how to make a Nutella sandwich.
3 No need to google it, that's definitely his name.
4 It's September 28th.
5 Mario Day covers all the characters in the Super Mario universe, though there was an attempt to get Columbus Day to be changed to recognise Luigi, a real American hero who was actually good at his job (unlike Columbus), but I am not sure that it was successful: www.change.org/p/congress-change-columbus-day-to-luigi-day
6 https://web.archive.org/web/20110708115131/http://www.capslockday.com

September 22nd: Hobbit Day – presumably a day when we have to think about all the injustices that happen to the inhabitants of the Shire, like coping with unwanted foot hair, being insanely obsessed with possessing a ring and having to fight off trolls. It's very like International Women's Day. There – I have written a joke that is both supportive of the feminist struggle and sexist at the same time.

October 22nd: CAPS LOCK DAY. NOT CONTENT WITH CELEBRATING THIS ONCE A YEAR, THE CAPS LOCK PEOPLE ALSO HAVE A SECOND DAY OF CELEBRATION. PERSONALLY, I WON'T BE HAPPY TILL WE DO IT EVERY DAY AND EVERYONE IS FORCED TO WRITE LIKE THIS ALL THE TIME. IT'S THE PUNISHMENT WE DESERVE.

December 22nd: Global Orgasm Day. Timed to coincide with the winter solstice, this is a day when everyone is encouraged to have an orgasm, while thinking of peace. I don't know about you, but that sounds like a difficult wank to me. If I can at least think of peace wearing a lacy bra then I think I can have a pop at it.

It's actually pretty hard to find something that doesn't have a day. Which is why I have invented a delightful parlour game called 'Does It Have A Day?' You can play it at Christmas with your family. All you need is a device with an internet connection and your imagination. You take it in turns to name a thing that you feel can't possibly have its own special day: it has to be a thing or a cause rather than a person as, strictly speaking, any individual person has a birthday, which would count as their day. Then you google whatever you've chosen.

If it turns out that it doesn't have a day then you get a point. If it does have a day (even tangentially) then you lose a point. It doesn't have to be a day recognised by the UN or one with its own Google Doodle. There just has to be a page about it somewhere online, meaning someone else has thought of it and (however lazily) tried to set it up.

The other players should also check the internet to find a way that your choice technically has a day. And then you can argue about it. It's brilliant fun.

To give you an example: I am at my desk and my drink is on a coaster. I am pretty certain there isn't a Coaster Day, but let's see if I am right. I am now googling 'Coaster Day'.

Ah, balls. First entry on Google is for National Roller Coaster Day, which is on August 16th. I know that that isn't what I meant, but that's what I said. I lose a point. I should have gone for Beer Mat Day. Which, incredibly, has not been invented. There isn't even a Mat Day. Though Mat Day is a carpenter in Norwich and also means asshole in Vietnamese. Mat Day's friends are going to be delighted about that when they read this book.

There *is* a Lumpy Rug Day,[1] which tries to encourage people to take better care of their floor coverings, but it

1 www.daysoftheyear.com/days/lumpy-rug-day

would take a genius to argue that that includes beer mats. You might get further with arguing that beer mats are covered by International Beer Day,[1] or Beer Day Britain,[2] as beer mats are surely part of the pub experience.

You can see how you could kill a few hours arguing the toss about stuff like this. Remember to then try to set up your winning day by choosing a date and making a website so no one can copy you and use it in a future game of Does It Have A Day?

The point I am making is that getting a day to celebrate something isn't a rare privilege or something to be envied.

Even if there wasn't an International Men's Day,[3] it would take only slightly more effort than tweeting 'What about International Men's Day?' to invent it.

Anyone can start a day, but how easy is it to make it popular enough to be celebrated?

Weirdly, that's the next question in the book.

1   First Friday of August.
2   June 15th: www.beerdaybritain.co.uk
3   Which there is. It's on November 19th.

@███████ Whens my wedding anniversary and first son's birthday?

| @Herring1967 November 19th

@███████ I see there's an International Women's Day, but when is Raymond Blanc's birthday?

| @Herring1967 November 19th

@███████ When is it exactly 6 weeks until Hogmanay?

| @Herring1967 November 19th

@███████ do you know when the 323rd day of the year is

| @Herring1967 November 19th

@███████ Rich, on what day in 1969 did Pele score his 1,000th goal?

| @Herring1967 November 19th

@███████ what date in 1942 was Mutesa II crowned 35th King of Buganda, prior to restoration of kingdom 1993?

| @Herring1967 Ask me a hard one. Nov 19

13

ANYONE CAN START A DAY, BUT HOW EASY IS IT TO MAKE IT POPULAR ENOUGH TO BE CELEBRATED?

International Men's Day has been going since 1992 (though it didn't really get under way until 1999) and International Women's Day arguably began in embryonic form in 1909 and has had over a century to bed in. Is it unreasonable to expect a relatively new day to get the traction of one that's been going for so long? How easy is it to start up a day that captures the public mood and is it possible to get there in just a couple of decades?

I have some experience of this because I have idly tried to start my own celebratory day. On a radio show at some point in the early 1990s, as a perennially unattached young man (because women are only attracted to bad guys and not because I was an immature idiot, like some people might say[1]), I railed against St Valentine, the patron saint of making sad, lonely people feel like shit. 'A day for love,' I might have tweeted, if that option had been available to me then. 'When will there be a day for the unloved?'

I proposed that in reaction to Valentine's Day,[2] we declare February 15th to be a celebration of hatred and the destruction of love, saucy greetings cards and people with girlfriends/boyfriends. If you see anyone even holding hands on this unholy day, you're allowed to push them both in a puddle. Anyone who's had sex this calendar year gets put in solitary confinement. If there's someone you really hate, you can send them an elaborate, expensive and anonymous card going into detail about why you think they're such a meatus. But the real selling point is this: if you're in a relationship that you're not happy about, you're allowed to just walk away from it, with no explanations, no repercussions, no reparations.

I named the day for the one person I thought really exemplified those ideals – St Skeletor. I know it's hard to believe that He-Man's nemesis was canonised, until you discover that it happened under Pope Boniface.[3]

---

1 Weirdly, the angrier I got about women not being interested in us good guys, the less interested in me they became, the shallow idiots.
2 14th February.
3 I don't write many proper jokes, but this is an absolute cracker – provided you fall within the intersection of the Venn diagram of people who are aware of the characters in *Masters of the Universe* and also have knowledge of obscure medieval popes. Sadly, I am the only person who does.

I have casually mentioned the idea a few times, including on my TV show in 1998[1] and my *Metro* newspaper column and blog. I will usually mention it on 15th February on social media, but I haven't made a concerted effort to publicise it.

Even so, if you google St Skeletor's Day you will find the day has gained a tiny bit of traction. It's acknowledged by the Urban Dictionary[2] and the renowned day-checking website checkiday.com[3] and there's a St Skeletor Day Facebook group with nearly 800 followers,[4] which, interestingly, doesn't mention me at all . . . Is the fact that the day has a life beyond me a sign that it's made a leap to the mainstream?

St Skeletor's Day even briefly had a Wikipedia page, until moderators decided it did not deserve one.[5] Moderator Uncle G (who has probably never created a special day in their life) commented in 2005, 'By next year, this will have been forgotten and *another* comedian will invent *another* 'anti-Valentine' Day.' Uncle G has quite a nerve.

But, most importantly, St Skeletor's Day has never had a Google Doodle and is not recognised by the UN, so I have to consider it a failure.

---

1 www.youtube.com/watch?v=vSHH4ih_KQY
2 www.urbandictionary.com/define.php?term=St%20Skeletor%27s%20Day
3 www.checkiday.com/a83dfe1018f24504dc6c7e731be47e6b/st-skeletors-day
4 www.facebook.com/StSkeletorsDay. Come on, let's see if we can push it over 1,000.
5 To find out why, head here: https://en.wikipedia.org/wiki/Wikipedia:
Articles_for_deletion/St_Skeletor%27s_Day. It's pretty hurtful.

I hate to prove Uncle G right, but a more successful, though less artful (though I would say that) response to Valentine's Day was created by Boston DJ[1] Tom Birdsey in 2002 when he declared March 14th Steak and Blowjob Day. Which, according to Wikipedia (yeah, all right, it got a Wikipedia entry and no one deleted it), is a day on which women are 'supposed to cook a filet steak for and perform fellatio on a man in response to cards, chocolates and flowers by men on Valentine's Day.'

Tom Birdsey didn't understand opposites! Valentine's Day is a day for lovers, not women. And you can choose what you have for dinner and unless you balls things up you're almost guaranteed to have sex too, so it's already steak and blowjob day. The opposite of love is hate, not blowjobs. Like Jeremy Corbyn, St Skeletor's Day wins the argument. But like Boris Johnson, Steak and Blowjob Day wins the actual competition. Proving anything with a BJ in it will always triumph.

I suspect that Tom was having a little bit of a laugh, though, and perhaps attempting to wind up feminists (and possibly vegetarians) with his crassness. He has been quite success-ful. Lois Banner, a professor of history at the University of Southern California, said it 'sounds like another part of the feminist backlash ... What we are moving toward in this culture is a very gross version of human interaction. This is

---

1   A DJ! Not a comedian like you thought it would be, Uncle G. Not so clever now, are you?

part of the hook-up culture. Most of my female students hate it, because they feel it is enforced by men.'

Sure, it would be pretty horrific and *Handmaids Tale*-y if Steak and Blowjob Day was mandatory, but I think it's a bit like complaining to Amnesty International about St Skeletor's Day's aims to imprison people for having relationships. Steak and Blowjob Day is a joke. Not as funny as my anti-love day, but funnier than saying, 'When's International Men's Day?'

Steak and Blowjob Day has probably got better name recognition than International Men's Day, though, and that's because it understands its audience better. Would you rather have a day where there's an outside possibility that your partner might cook for you and gob you off or think about why so many young men are committing suicide?

I seriously wonder if Tom Birdsey's day rather than International Women's Day is the reason International Men's Day fails to capture public imagination.

@█████ I'm so looking forward to international Men's day . . .

> @Herring1967 Me too, what have you got planned for November 19th?

@█████ Why aren't there banners hung around town on international men's day?

> @Herring1967 Cos you can't be arsed to put them up?

@█████ Is there an International Men's Day?

> @Herring1967 Hi, there is. It's on November 19th. Let me know if you're interested in helping out with the organisation and what I can put you down for on the day.

@█████ Is there an International Men's Day? Legit question

> @Herring1967 And one with an incredibly easy to find answer. November 19th. What will you do with this info? Legit question.

@█████ Perhaps if international men's day was given a higher profile . . .

> @Herring1967 All it takes is for men to give a fuck about it. Who do you think is promoting IWD?

@Herring1967 If only we could harness all this power and anger and put into actual IMD, imagine how big it would be.

14

WHY DOESN'T INTERNATIONAL MEN'S DAY GET THE SAME SUPPORT AS INTERNATIONAL WOMEN'S DAY?

During my annual International 'When's International Men's Day?' Day marathon I am quite regularly told that, OK, it's true there is an International Men's Day, but it doesn't get the same level of attention and media interest as International Women's Day. In fact, that's the reason that so many men ask about it, because no one tells them it exists. QED.

This is a slightly circular argument because, despite my telling literally thousands of people about the date, it does not seem to have inspired any of them to take part in the actual day.

Analysis of Google searches (yes, some people do think to use a search engine rather than just moan on social media) shows a spike in searches for International Men's Day on

March 8th (it's the most searched term on that day, in spite of it being International Women's Day), but there's not much interest for the rest of the year.

When replying to the question, I have often asked what the questioner is going to do on the day, and even if they want to meet up and do something with me, but not a single one has replied. It's like they think I'm weird or something.

Maybe they need time to think how they are going to mark the day.

I put this to the test in 2019 and added an extra dimension to my Twitter marathon. As well as informing everyone who asked when International Men's Day was,[1] I doubled my workload by writing a scheduled tweet to the same people, to arrive on November 19th, with words to the effect of, 'It's today! What have you got planned?'

Not one of them bothered to get back in touch on the day itself. It might be because they were too busy taking part in the huge parade they'd organised celebrating masculine positivity, but if so the biased feminist media didn't even report it. Typical.

Imagine if the energy men put into complaining about there being no International Men's Day was put in to celebrating International Men's Day.

Men are aggrieved that there is no day, but also expect someone else to do all the hard work in setting it up. I

---

1 November 19th.

sometimes joke that the reason International Men's Day isn't as widely celebrated as International Women's Day is because we can't expect women to organise it all for us. Probably most of the men complaining are used to their mum organising stuff for them.

The truth is, of course, that there are various events set up to celebrate men on November 19th, but most men (even the ones furious about a day not existing, even though it does exist) don't seem to be interested in taking part. Absolutely no one is stopping men celebrating International Men's Day, so why aren't they doing so?

It reminds me of what happens in England on April 23rd, St George's Day. There's exactly the same kind of disgruntled mumbling about how the English aren't allowed to celebrate their national day in the same way as their neighbours in Wales, Scotland and Ireland. Usually the conclusion is that it's due to political correctness gone mad and it wouldn't be allowed.

But is anyone actively stopping St George's Day celebrations? The tabloids certainly think so. Take this headline from the *Daily Mirror* of April 29th 2010:

ST GEORGE'S FLAG BAN ON TAXIS IN THURROCK

Wow. In Thurrock, it seems, taxi drivers were not allowed to celebrate being English. But is there more to this than meets the eye?

Patriotic taxi drivers have been banned from flying St George's Cross flags from their cars.

This is awful.

Cabbies flew them to celebrate the patron saint of England's day last week. But police acting on council orders in Thurrock, Essex, later ordered the drivers to remove them.

You can understand the tabloid fury. They wouldn't let us English celebrate being English. Except the article then goes on to say:

A council spokesman said flags, along with adverts, breached taxi licences. But he added: 'In the spirit of St George's Day, we were happy to let them display the flags but they had to remove them after the event.'

Oh, right. It turns out that the ban was nothing to do with prejudice. It was to do with regulations about advertising – and they actually let them have the flags anyway. So the headline could have read:

BAN ON ADVERTISING LIFTED TO

CELEBRATE ENGLISHNESS

Maybe people don't want to celebrate St George's Day because the day can be hijacked by flag-waving racists, or because there is some residual guilt over England's history with all the unpleasantness of the crusades, the empire and what we did to that poor old Australian, Braveheart, all of which is at odds with our multicultural present. Celebrating being the oppressor has a very different feel to uniting because you were the ones being oppressed.

Or maybe it's because Englishness means different things to different people, and can't be represented by the stereotype projected by the media or the nostalgic vision laid out by Nigel Farage.

So what is Englishness?

England is a country originally created by invasion of northern Europeans, our patron saint is the son of a Roman and Palestinian, our flag is copied off the Genoans, our royal banner is three lions (animals indigenous to Africa), the figurehead of the Church of England is a Palestinian Jew, we have a German royal family, our national food is curry and we have citizens from pretty much every nation of the earth.

Being a man is a similarly complex combination of factors, and just as many English people don't feel they conform to the St George's Day English template, many men are probably put off International Men's Day because of what they imagine the stereotypical celebrant must be like. I think that this embarrassing and possibly unfair stereotype is created in some large degree by the men who ask *that* question on

March 8th. They make International Men's Day feel like it is some kind of answer to International Women's Day, a feeling which is in essence misogynist and one that most men find a bit embarrassing, because they like women. They all came out of one.

There's definitely something about the day that is putting men off, given that Steak and Blowjob Day (which really should be way more embarrassing) gets more publicity and has successfully entered the public consciousness.

More tellingly, there's another November endeavour which men have enthusiastically supported; an endeavour designed specifically to make people consider the big issues affecting men – testicular and prostate cancer, mental health and suicide prevention: Movember.

Combining facial hair and humour even more successfully than I did with a Hitler moustache, this whole month of support for men has gone from strength to strength since it was established in 2003. What could be more fun than attempting to grow a moustache every November? You've got the perfect excuse in that you're doing something for a good cause, so it doesn't matter if you look stupid.

It's positive, it's funny and it's inclusive, too, welcoming Mo Bros and Mo Sistas, because, as much as society wants us to believe otherwise, women are mammals too and thus hairy. It covers all the things that the International Women's Day complainers claim are never addressed, and gets all kinds of media coverage. Plus it's not just a day, it's a *whole month*.

Growing embarrassing facial hair and pretending you're going to get oral sex obviously resonates with men more than the passive-aggressiveness (and often aggressive-aggressiveness) of International Men's Day. Or at least the perception of International Men's Day.

Should we just throw our weight behind Movember or is there an argument for still highlighting men on the 19th, when our moustaches have hopefully stopped being scratchy? And are we right to view International Men's Day the way we do?

@█████ what date is International Men's Day this year?

@Herring1967 I don't think they change the date. It would be confusing. Hopefully they will stick to November 19th or I am going to look quite the Charlie.

@█████ Not so gentle reminder : On Last international men's day not even a single person wished me or anyone i know, so i promised not to wish anyone on #internationalwomensday so i am keeping things equal as promised. expect no tweets about women's day! #genderequalitydoneright

@Herring1967 Can everyone please set up a scheduled tweet for Pedro, wishing him Happy International Men's Day on 19th November?

@█████ Unfortunately, I doubt you'll ever see an international men's day, even though men built society.

@Herring1967 No, there is one, even though women built us, and it's on November 19th.

@█████ Malangnya takde siapa kesah kalau esok adalah International Men's day huhuhu ~

This is what all the IMD tweets look like to me by this stage

15

WHAT'S INTERNATIONAL MEN'S DAY?

Now that's a better question. Why is no one asking *what* instead of *when*? Why has it taken me until nearly the end of the book to come to that myself?

The first International Men's Day was in 1992 and inaugurated by Thomas Oaster from the Missouri Center for Men's Studies at the University of Missouri–Kansas City. It was celebrated in the three main countries in the world: USA, Australia and Malta.

And do you know what date it was held on?

WRONG! It was February 7th.

Oh bugger. I've given everyone the wrong date. I am going to have to send them all a corrected tweet. Bear with me . . .

What a twist! I hope your mind is blown. Forget everything you have learned.

And then relearn it again, because although the original International Men's Day celebrations petered out after just three years (except in Malta where they've been going since 1994), the day was revived in 1999 in Trinidad and Tobago by Dr Jerome Teelucksingh of the University of the West Indies.

And what date did he choose? WARNING: this could be a trick question.

It isn't a trick. It was November 19th. Hooray – all is right with the world again. You can't have that many twists or your readers will expire from shock.

Excuse me, I just have to tweet everyone again again.

World Toilet Day wasn't going to exist for another two years. Jerome got there first. The toilets should have chosen another day. Men were here first. Which is also true of men and toilets in general.

Charmingly, Dr Teelucksingh chose November 19th not only because it was his dad's birthday, but also because it was the tenth anniversary of the day that Trinidad and Tobago nearly got into the World Cup finals. But didn't. Because they lost 1-0 to the USA.

When asked about his motivation for starting the day, Dr Teelucksingh said, 'I realized there was no day for men ... some have said that there is Father's Day but what about young boys, teenagers and men who are not fathers?'

What is notable about this is that the whole thing didn't begin because someone thought: 'International Women's Day? When's International Men's Day?'

Dr Teelucksingh appears genuinely to have wanted a day for men – not because there was one for women, but simply because one didn't exist already.

The origin is borne out by the aims of the day. In 2009, the IMD Coordination Committee ratified their core objectives (the so-called Six Pillars), which you can still read on the time-capsuled IMD website[1] (which really makes you appreciate how far website design has come in the last decade).

1. To promote positive male role models; not just movie stars and sportsmen but everyday, working-class men who are living decent, honest lives.
2. To celebrate men's positive contributions to society, community, family, marriage, child care, and to the environment.
3. To focus on men's health and wellbeing; social, emotional, physical and spiritual.
4. To highlight discrimination against males; in areas of social services, social attitudes and expectations, and law.
5. To improve gender relations and promote gender equality.
6. To create a safer, better world; where people can be safe and grow to reach their full potential.

---

1 https://sites.google.com/a/imd-global.org/international-mens-day/about-imd

None of those have a knee-jerk, anti-women vibe, do they? In fact, it's a pretty reasonable summing up of the areas in life where men are struggling, and recognises the importance of gender equality in making a better world for 'people', wherever they fall on the spectrum of gender. It doesn't feel like a furious response to International Women's Day so much as an extension pack, coming at the same problems from the other side.

My own prejudices against the day come from the idiots who use it as an excuse to try and disrupt International Women's Day. But, at the heart of it, is International Men's Day actually about something different? Are my own uneasy feelings about it solely down to the internet trolls trying to turn it into a stupid competition?

Might International Men's Day be worth celebrating?

You might have thought it weird that the chosen date commemorates a sporting defeat. It's not your usual dunder-headed macho bullshit where only victory counts. The Trinidad and Tobago match is a wonderful symbol of a country coming together. The team only needed a draw to progress to the World Cup finals, but they were beaten 1-0.

The fact that the day commemorates a day, not of sporting victory, but of a noble reaction to defeat is what I like best about the choice of date. Their dreams were shattered, yet still they celebrated. The 65,000 spectators (in a stadium that was supposed to have a capacity of under 30,000) were awarded the FIFA Fair Play Award for 1989 because of their reaction.

The date of International Men's Day was chosen as a tribute to a father and to a community working together, so it's a shame if anyone (on either side[1]) is using it as a way to create division.

---

1 Yes, including me.

@░░░░░░ @BBCSport When is international men's day or did I miss it?

> @Herring1967 You haven't missed it this year, It's November 19th. But sadly you have missed all the ones over the last two to three decades. You should probably pay more attention in future.

@░░░░░░ Just throwing this out there. When's international men's day?

> @Herring1967 ~let me lob it back with November 19th written on it.

@░░░░░░ When's International men's day?

> @Herring1967 Ben is educated at Oxford and Cambridge according to his bio. Proving degrees from those places aren't worth wiping your arse on. November 19th, Ben. November 19th.

@░░░░░░ International Women's Day today. Is there an International Men's Day?

> @Herring1967 I've been trying to find out too, cos it's a good question. I don't know how we'll find out though, let me know if you have any ideas.

16

WHEN'S WHITE HISTORY MONTH?

Earlier in the book I decided I didn't need to explain why it was ridiculous to ask the question 'When's White History Month?' I hoped it was obvious.

But while writing this book I've witnessed some unbelievable responses to the Black Lives Matter protests and I think they need addressing. It's like 'When's International Men's Day?' magnified a thousand times, and I think it helps us to understand the motivations of the people who feel the need to flip the narrative whenever they suspect they are being excluded.

I do wonder how many people who say 'All Lives Matter' or, something I thought I'd never see, 'White Lives Matter' started off asking about International Men's Day. Did they enjoy the feeling they got from challenging International Women's Day and then go on to the harder stuff? Could

'When's International Men's Day?' be the gateway drug that leads to the dangerous (and brain-damaging) stuff?

So let's ask another question that I had assumed didn't need an answer: why don't we have a White History Month?

Clearly, one of the main reasons we have Black History Month is to attempt to address the fact that the history we are predominantly (and maybe exclusively) taught is of white people.

At school, the only time that I can recall any mention of black people in a history lesson was in the one about how great William Wilberforce was for abolishing the slave trade. So even that lesson was really about the white guy. Similarly the classes on the Scramble for Africa largely overlooked who exactly was being scrambled over (and robbed, raped and murdered – why do I keep using parentheses to do this?)

It's impressive how white-centric our history is, given that Homo sapiens have been around for about 200,000 years and the white-coloured variant only appeared around 8,000 years ago. And even now they only account for about a quarter of the world's population.

What would you even do during White History Month? I guess we'd have to highlight all the other UK royal personages from history and stop filling the history books with the exploits of Meghan Markle.

From White History Month, it's just a short step to responding to 'Black Lives Matter' with 'All Lives Matter'. Black Lives Matter is not an assertion that white lives don't, it's just an appeal to the world to realise that you are on the receiving end of a huge and life-threatening injustice if you are black. To give one tiny example: one in a thousand black American men will die at the hands of the police.[1] That's around 3.5 times more likely than a white person being killed by a cop.[2]

Some people who say 'All Lives Matter' claim they are making a point about equality, that it's only bad individual cops who are killing black people. But when a system employs that many 'bad individuals' and the statistics are that bleak then surely you have to start blaming the system?

Just like many International 'When's International Men's Day?' Day wazzocks, you might believe your question isn't based on prejudice. But it is.

When I looked at the kind of men who thought it was worth congregating in central London to protest against Black Lives Matter, it really brought home to me the crisis at the heart of modern-day masculinity. They were dubbed by the press as anti-anti-fascists (just like the non-non-wazzocks discussed earlier), as if it were possible to be against anti-fascists without actually being a fascist. As if these men felt so strongly about freedom of speech that they were out there protesting for the right for people to be fascist, even though they weren't fascist themselves.

---

1 www.pnas.org/content/116/34/16793
2 https://www.theguardian.com/us-news/2020/jul/14/
    donald-trump-george-floyd-police-killings

It was a distinction that was a little let down by some of the protestors apparently giving Nazi salutes, squaring up to policemen and picnickers because there was no one else to fight and one of them urinating on a memorial to a victim of terrorism.

These men are angry at something, but they don't know what, exactly. It's easier for them to blame people who are different to them than it is to blame themselves, or more pertinently the system that has encouraged them to bottle up their feelings and made them dispensable.

Is it wrong to want to help those over-sensitive, lost men, fighting against anyone they can over something they can't even define? It feels counter-intuitive, if you care about equality, to pay any mind to those who are actively protesting against it. But is helping them to work out who they are actually an important step in achieving equality? If you convince people not to be racist or sexist then wouldn't that actually put an end to racism and sexism?

Might International Men's Day be able to get us a little closer to that goal?

@████████ @LewisHamilton WHAT DAY IS INTERNATIONAL MEN'S DAY?

> @Herring1967 Why are you bothering Lewis Hamilton with this? He is a very busy man. It's TUESDAY (19th November. Good luck with driving that car around in loads of circles again Lewis (know how you must feel)

@████ @Apple @Beyonce Did I miss international men's day?

> @Herring1967 Yup. But it'll be round again on November 19th. If you're trying to impress @beyonce then I'm not sure it's working.

@██████ @10DowningStreet @theresa_may and 5 others When is international men's day?

> @Herring1967 The PM is very busy fucking up Brexit so please don't waste her time on stuff like this. It's November 19th. When's Brexit? That's a better question for her.

@█████ @EmWatson tell me, when is it international mens day?

> @Herring1967 @EmWatson November 19th. Hello Emma. We have the same sized hands[1]

@Herring1967 Just to preempt you @realDonaldTrump, it's November 19th

---

1 We really do. I put my hands in her hand-prints at Harry Potter World and they were a perfect fit.

17

WHAT IS A MAN?

Most logical people are sceptical about horoscopes. Surely you can't really divide the whole human race up into twelve personality types based on the month they were born in? Come on.

Yet people often seem happy to divide the world into two kinds of people based on whether their genitalia is an inny or an outy.[1]

If I started doing that with belly buttons you'd think I was crazy, but that's not going to stop me. Inny belly buttoners are kind, reliable, sensitive and nurturing and outies are selfish, violent monsters who hate us inny norms. I'm only saying what we're all thinking.

We hold stereotypes of all kinds of people, and these

---

1   Even though gender is actually much more complex than that.

stereotypes are usually negative or at least patronising. What I find astonishing is that men are the only group I can think of who not only rarely complain about their pigeon-holing, but instead actively embrace it and even try to live up to it.

I once saw an American female comedian who said something along the lines of: 'Men! They're selfish, they're bad parents, they're lazy, they're drunks, they care more about sports and cars than they do about us and they always lie to us ... and we wouldn't have it any other way, would we, girls?'

Both men and women in the audience cheered and laughed. I didn't recognise myself in that description (although, to be fair, I was a bit drunk at the time) and I felt it was weird that this comedian and the women in the audience were encouraging the men who fitted this awful cliché to carry on as they were.

There wasn't even a groan of protest from the men present (which you'd definitely get if you said something even playfully judgemental about pretty much any other group). I was affronted, but didn't protest either (I was also on the bill that night so it might have looked unprofessional).

I don't believe the majority of men are like that, so why are some men happy to excuse the behaviour of the men who make us all look bad and the system that fucks so many of us up?

Notions of masculinity vary so much both historically and culturally that it's nonsensical to talk about it in absolute terms. There's a notion that is the central argument of another comedy show that left me cold and feeling excluded – *Defending the Caveman* by Rob Becker – that men can't help behaving the way they do because of traits we evolved as lone and inarticulate hunters in prehistoric times, whilst women are more sociable because their DNA is hard-wired to gathering berries and looking after the kids.

Even if any of that were true, it'd be no excuse to behave the same way now, unless you were also happy to shit in a bush while defending yourself against lions with a stick and no longer use Deliveroo.

No one really knows what gender roles were in prehistoric times, but many experts now believe they might have been a lot more equal than is generally assumed. Mark Dyble of University College London, who has studied modern hunter-gatherer tribes, which generally operate on an egalitarian basis, suggested: 'Sexual equality is one of an important suite of changes to social organisation, including things like pair-bonding, our big, social brains, and language, that distinguishes humans.' It's possible that the agricultural revolution and the consequent accumulation of resources led to our more patriarchal society, and it's not definitively our natural state. On the other hand, chimps live in male-dominated societies and (aside from the ones who advertised PG Tips) none of them have ever amounted to anything. It's possible that the human race owes its success to equality.

It seems weird to argue that our societal structures are

unchanging and date from thousands of years ago and then ignore the variety of masculine ideals that have come since. You don't see many people arguing that part of manliness is having sex with adolescent boys, but some evidence shows that's what the Ancient Greeks believed. Nor do I see many modern men emulating the medieval notion of chivalry or even the 1950s notion of holding open doors for women. The masculine role is ever-changing, both historically and culturally, and we can't keep looking backwards or arguing that it is immutable.

We need to adapt to a world where men are in danger of redundancy. We are being replaced by machines at work, by drones and missiles at war and by turkey basters in the family (women can get rid of us provided they keep a few men willing to be milked for gametes – I'm very much up for it). We need to up our game, and we need to stop defending the system and the stereotypes that make most of us dispensable and blaming our worst excesses on some fanciful ideas of prehistoric roles.

Men aren't Neanderthals, and by seeing them as such we ignore those of us who have created beautiful art and music, world-changing ideas, built buildings, crafted wood and stone. We're ignoring the amazing fathers, the incredible lovers, the men who have used their strength to fight oppression. And the ones who have combined their knowledge of He-Man and medieval popes to create an unbeatable pun.

I am not denying the bad things that men can do (in fact

I've been banging on about it in parentheses for the entire book), nor am I saying we don't have anything to apologise for or anything we need to change. We're not unevolved apes, so why are we defining ourselves by the worst of us?

Being a man (and being a human) means you are part of an incredible spectrum of personalities, lifestyles, sexualities and gender. There is absolutely nothing that completely unites men apart from the feeling that we are men.

Some of us are hiding who we really are, for fear of being judged by the 'proper' men, perhaps because we've been taught it's not manly to express our feelings. But I don't think those proper men are proper men, either. They're nearly all pretending for exactly the same reasons.

My own personal theory[1] is that those men who most live up to the stereotype of masculinity (and indeed those women who most live up to the stereotype of femininity) are the most insecure about it all. And the insane levels of confidence that men feel they must exhibit to qualify for the club are part of the same deal.

We need to build up the confidence to be who we actually are.

In 2001 I was doing a stand-up show in the same theatre as a production of *The Vagina Monologues* and I thought to myself, 'That's a bit sexist. When will there be a *Vagina Monologues* for men?'

---

1 Which, obviously, I have no evidence for.

I am nothing if not a hypocrite.

But, unlike the When's International Men's Day brigade, I didn't just sit back and moan, I wrote a stage show and a book called *Talking Cock* to examine men's relationship with their yoghurt-spitting sausage and their own masculinity.

Initially I'd thought this show was redundant, given that men do pretty much nothing else but talk about their spam javelins, but I soon realised that they rarely do so seriously. I set up an anonymous online questionnaire that revealed that many many men harboured concerns and fears that they are generally too scared to discuss.

The defining moment happened one night after the show when I was on stage clearing my props after the audience had filed out of the theatre. A tough-looking guy with a beard and tattoos came into the auditorium and told me he was looking for his cigarettes. After a cursory look around he said to me quietly, 'You know that bit about snapping the banjo string? [referring to a section on penile injury and how the frenulum, the tag of skin between the foreskin and the shaft of the penis, can tear] I thought I was the only one that had happened to.' A weight appeared to have lifted from his shoulders and he left – without the cigarettes that he had 'lost'.

He'd never been able to talk to anyone about this incident and consequently felt alone.

Men needed a show where their genitals were honestly discussed just as much as women did, and I realise now that men also need a day where they can share their personal experiences of being a man.

But when will there ever be a day like that?

@████████ There isn't an international men's day, equality?????????

> @Herring1967 There is. November 19th. Happy?????????

@Herring1967 Just fell asleep for a bit with my hands still on my keyboard. Luckily I woke before becoming mummified (sorry meninists – daddified)

@████████ Correct me if I'm wrong but we have int women's days but I don't remember international men's day

> @Herring1967 You are wrong. Nov 19

@Herring1967 Might be time for a little break November 19th. November 19th.November 19th. November 19th.November 19th. November 19th. November 19th. November 19th.November 19th. November 19th.November 19th. November 19th. November 19th. November 19th.November 19th. November 19th.November 19th. All November 19th and no play makes Rich a dull boy

@Herring1967 I hate you world. I am instituting a Destroy humanity day. It's November 18th. Just so those fuckers don't get a day.

18

COULD WE MAKE INTERNATIONAL MEN'S DAY A THING?

When I first started replying to the question 'When's International Men's Day?' I was pretty much of the opinion that International Men's Day itself was something we didn't actually need.[1] Men already ruled the world, right?

I've changed my mind.

A day for a thing or a cause (whether International or National, recognised by the UN and Google or not, serious or frivolous) is not really that big a deal. It's just an opportunity to have a think and maybe a chat about an issue. That issue can be whether you think Nutella tastes nice or what we can do to stop human trafficking. Obviously one of those issues is way more important than the other,

---

1   Even though it exists and is on November 19th.

but luckily we are capable of caring about more than one thing at once.

None of these days are compulsory. If it's not your bag,[1] you don't have to get involved.

For me, the issues faced by women fighting for equality are greater than those faced by men. But the issues faced by black people are greater still. Does that mean I shouldn't care about women? Or men? Of course not. I can care about all that *and* Nutella. I have the capacity to be interested in and concerned about thousands of things.

Men deserve a day, and they need it, too. Men need to talk to each other and about each other and to speak up about the injustices that they are facing (largely from other men – you get what the brackets are about by now) but, more importantly, they need to celebrate the positives of being a man.

Let's not make it a day to complain too much about the bad things – we've got the whole month of Movember to raise awareness for that. If we're going to celebrate International Men's Day then we don't have to organise parades or worry about the event being covered by the media. It can be as simple as hell.

It's all laid out for us in those six pillars of the International Men's Day Coordination Committee. We should be:

---

1   If bags are your bag, National Handbag Day is October 10th.

1. Praising positive male role models: let's talk up the men who have been doing things right. I'm going to post a big picture of Sir Michael Palin on Twitter. Who do *you* think deserves the accolade?

2. Celebrating men's positive contributions to society: the stuff that matters, like our dad (if he was a good one) or the people of Trinidad and Tobago who danced in the face of defeat – the two inspirations for this day.

3. Focusing on men's wellbeing: ring up a friend you think might be struggling. Have a chat. For one day forget about the banter. Tell him you care about him. Ask him if he's ever snapped his banjo string.

4. Highlighting discrimination against males – and ascertain who it is who is actually responsible for this discrimination.

5. Improving gender relations and promoting gender equality: we have to create a fairer world together. The world belongs to us all and equality will benefit everyone. Women are welcome to join in our day (as long as for one day they stop banging on about their own bloody day – am I right, fellas?)

6. Creating a safer, better world: if we're strong let's use that strength to protect, if we're smart then let's use our brains for the common good, if we're nerds, let's see if we can help everyone with their computer problems. If we're funny (and that's basically all we have going for us), then let's try and make people laugh.

If men put even a quarter of the energy used to complain about International Women's Day into celebrating International Men's Day, then this thing could be HUGE.

And your mums aren't going to organise it for you, fellas. You have to do it yourselves.

@████████ Wait, when is international men's day??? #equality

> @Herring1967 It will never end. This will never end . . . November 19th

@████████ So . . . Is international men's day a thing?

> @Herring1967 YES YES IT FUCKING IS . . . Sorry you may have caught me at a bad time.

@████████ Soooo when is international men's day? These are things that I need to be aware of.

> @Herring1967 YOU THINK? DO YOU THINK SO? But how would you find out? Realistically? How would you find out if you needed to be aware of it? I mean no one has three seconds to spare to use google do they. Especially after they've wasted probably a minute composing a fucking tweet. 19/11

@████████ Where's international men day talk about unfair

> @Herring1967 Do you know what is unfair. Spending nine years letting people know about International Men's day and you still not having

a fucking clue. November 19th OK!!!!! Hope that helps make up for the prejudice you have had to face

@Herring1967 I am broken. I am sitting in a corner just saying Nov 19th over and over again and I can't remember why or what it means

19

HOW DO WE STOP PEOPLE ASKING ABOUT INTERNATIONAL MEN'S DAY ON INTERNATIONAL WOMEN'S DAY?

This small book touches upon some huge issues, but it has only one purpose and is only trying to change one thing. It is the tiniest of steps and in many ways it is a frivolous one. But it might prove to be a significant one.

It's trying to achieve what I attempted and failed to achieve over nine March 8ths – to stop men asking 'When's International Men's Day?' on International Women's Day.

That's it.

It's not much. But if that's all I achieved in my lifetime I'd be happy. If my gravestone just read, 'It's November 19th', that would be enough for me. It would be particularly apt if I died on November 19th. But I don't want to get greedy.

There are two good reasons to stop asking that one question (and just for one day):

1. It undermines International Women's Day.
2. It undermines International Men's Day.

If the people asking the question really care about International Men's Day then they need to know that they are damaging it. If they don't care about it and just have a problem with women having a day of celebration, then the damage is inside them and they need to address it. Women are not the reason their life is going the way it is. Their problems are likely caused by the same system that the women are fighting.

How do we stop it?

If you hear someone asking that question on International Women's Day, call them out on it, politely, but firmly.

Tell them, 'It's on November 19th. We've got eight months to work out what we're going to do and what aspect of men we want to celebrate.'

If they say, 'But why does no one care about male suicide, mental health and homelessness?'

Tell them: 'It's OK, all those issues have their own day and are also covered very effectively by Movember which is actually an entire month. But don't let the women find out. They only get a day. You know what they are like when they think something's not equal.'

If they say, 'But can't you see that society is sexist . . . it's sexist against men.'

You can reply, 'I love the face you're pulling, but I am not as surprised as you think about that opinion.'

If they still keep going on about International Men's Day then say, 'Look, we can talk about this on any other day. Just today is International Women's Day. Are there no women in your life that you want to celebrate? Your mother? Your sister? Your daughter? Your niece? Victoria Wood? Malala? Marie Curie? Oprah Winfrey? That woman who played in the darts finals?[1] Let's make today about women so we can make our day about men . . . Plus, you do realise that if women achieve equality, then men get to be equal too, right?'

Then pull a face like you have blown their mind. Because you might have.

If they still don't get it, I don't know what to suggest. Maybe buy them a copy of this book.

Thanks for reading. I hope I never have to write 'November 19th' again.

Oh, I don't know if you know. That's when International Men's Day is, by the way.

What have you got planned?

---

1 I apologise for repeatedly using her as a punchline. Her name is Fallon Sherrock and she is absolutely amazing.

@Herring1967 International Men's Day was in your heart all along . . . and also on November 19th

QUIZ

The test to see if you were paying attention:

1. Is there an International Men's Day?
   Yes/no [delete as applicable]

2. If so, when is it?

ACKNOWLEDGEMENTS

I would like to thank, first and foremost, my editor Rhiannon Smith. It was her idea to turn my day of stupidity into a book and to broaden its scope. I am also very grateful to Deborah Frances-White, both for allowing me to quote her at length and agreeing to take part in the audiobook, Nathan Caton for giving permission for me to mention his brilliant Twitter video and Catherine Wilkins for letting me use her joke, providing me with fantastic feedback on the book and possibly more importantly looking after the kids when deadlines got crazy (they're her kids too so it's not weird). And to Alistair Green for brilliantly bringing the tweets to life in the audiobook. Thanks to everyone at Sphere who gave me terrific support and encouragement at every stage, including Cath Burke, Thalia Proctor, Celeste Ward-Best, Kirsteen Astor and Marie Hrynczak (maybe employ some men next time, what about equality?). Also thanks to Nico Taylor for designing the cover. And many thanks to Katie Mckay, Dan Lloyd and Perrine Davari at Avalon.

And a huge shout out to the brilliant team at Refuge and especially Gabi Field. They deserve all the support and money that you can give them. They do fabulous, important and sadly necessary work and I am in awe of them. refuge.org.uk

'Perhaps if Michael Parkinson had asked Mohammad Ali if he'd ever seen a Bigfoot he might be remembered as a great interviewer. Instead it is Richard Herring who has perfected the art of creating funny, interesting and offensive questions that will supercharge even the dullest encounter'

Adam Buxton

'Would you rather read this book cover to cover every day for the rest of your life, or never read again? We would take the former, because it's the stupidest funniest book of the stupidest funniest questions we've ever read'

Elis James and John Robins

'Thank god and all her sisters for Richard Herring, leaving no turnable stone unimagined with these iceberg breakers'

Al Murray

'With this hysterical book, you will once again become the heart and soul of any gathering without having to take your trousers off or write self-loathing apology texts the next day'

Rufus Hound

'Of all the clever people I know, Richard is the stupidest. And of all the stupid people I know, Richard is the cleverest. That's why this is such a brilliant book for everyone'

Richard Osman

'Guaranteed to get a conversation started ... even if it ends up being a conversation about your weird taste in books'

Dave Gorman

'This book is very funny. And a social lifesaver. I'm definitely going to use it for my next awkward conversation with Richard Herring'
Sarah Millican

'Most of this book is pointless filth, all of it is hilarious, and my answer to question 715(a) is "Yes thank you and it was very tasty".'
Dawn French

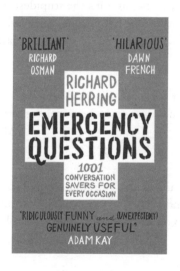

'I am involved in emergency situations on a daily basis, with Richard's book I can avoid the majority turning into crisis'
Bob Mortimer

'A perfect way to pretend you're interested in people you're not that interested in'
Kathy Burke